Klondike Playboy

Klondike Playboy

A MARINE HELICOPTER PILOT'S ANTICS AND
ADVENTURES FROM
PARRIS ISLAND TO VIET NAM

John Boden

Library of Congress Control Number: 2010909342
ISBN: Hardcover   978-1-4535-2672-9
                Softcover   978-1-4535-2671-2
                Ebook   978-1-4535-2673-6

This book was printed in the United States of America.

Find more photos and links at **www.klondikeplayboy.com**

To order additional copies of this book, contact:
Xlibris Corporation
1-888-795-4274
www.Xlibris.com
Orders@Xlibris.com
83161

Contents

Dedication

This book is dedicated to my children, my grandchildren and their children so that they may more easily learn to understand themselves by knowing their family roots.

And with special thanks to my wife Pat, the love of my life, who encouraged me, read, reread and corrected my thousands of misspellings and typos while repeatedly asking, "Where is the part about me?"

Introduction

I don't know why you would want to read a book about a part of my life. You probably have never heard of me; I am not famous and I never did anything that was a great benefit to the world.

Maybe you are like me, just doing what you do each day as it unfolds when you get up in the morning. Maybe you will find parts of yourself in me. Maybe you will share a laugh with me. Maybe you will have a small taste while reading it of the wonderful and fun time I had writing it.

Whatever, I thank you for reading it, and I hope it will bring you a smile.

Truth Ferments with Age

I am an adherent to the standard of truth used by the court. Always tell the truth, the whole truth, and nothing but the truth. But, as I have started the process of writing about the stories that have made my life the great trip that it is, I am finding that my adherence to my standard of truth is showing cracks and other structural flaws. As I look back, there seems to be a blurriness that has removed the sharp edges and details. It is easy to assure you that I am not lying, that the events did occur and that I am always telling the truth, but I am also sure that it is not always the whole truth or nothing but the truth. I can't remember the whole truth of what happened forty, fifty or even sixty years ago. I am also pretty sure that, as I wander around in the telling of not only the story, but also the circumstances surrounding it, I am telling more than the truth. By that I mean how the factors in all memory systems, such as things with an emotional impact, are stored. They seem to be remembered in what are crisp and detailed pictures. But are we sure those pictures are really accurate or that the fish really weighed that much?

If for some reason you are forced to spend some of your valuable time reading my ramblings, and if any of you who were involved with or were witness to any of the times described and you remember things differently, please understand that my memory has fermented and aged. The stories are what I remember and are my truth, as I am sure you have your truth. For example, when my brother and I are together telling a story about a shared childhood event to our children and grandchildren, it is sometimes hard for anyone to believe that we were both there at the same place and time, since we spend as much or more time in correcting and adding to the other's version of the story as in its actual telling.

Writing the stories brings me a big advantage as I can record them the way I remember them without having to bend to the constant meddling of others trying to assist me in the telling of it, unless, of course, I agree that their viewpoint is more accurate and makes for a better story. To make the telling flow more easily, I sometimes use a file to round the sharp edges and pointed corners and putty to fill in the cracks and voids. And the reason I am bashing my head, gnashing my teeth and taking the time trying to get the memories onto paper is that I am telling myself my story. In a way I am much more concerned that *I* enjoy the writing and the memories that float up in the process, than in *your* enjoying the reading of them. I had one hell of a lot of fun and adventure in my life and, as I enter my dotage, I love being able to have it again in my memory. My memory, or what is still left of it, seems to have also created a fog around a lot of my toils and troubles that weren't anywhere as much fun as as the good times. Another great benefit of a fermenting memory!

I also periodically use people's names when I remember them and it helps the story. My memory issues will have a more direct effect on them, as, like my brother, they may wonder how I could have gotten the details so botched up. If you are a person I didn't mention in a story and you wish I had, I apologize, and I also accept your thanks if you are happy I didn't mention your name.

In any Marine Corps stories where I refer to rank, you may notice it usually has a negative spin on it. Yes, I did serve with some excellent leaders of field grade (Major and above). Most of the majors that met this standard were on their way through to more responsible positions and higher rank. There are some references to the few I held in high esteem in one or two stories. The others, I will have to admit, remind me that the word "rank" itself has two meanings, *double entendre*, if you will. Do they produce a foul odor, have more grade, or, as is often the case, both? This fine point allowed me to have an innocence glowing from my face whenever a person of rank gave me one of those looks that says "Did you just insult me?" that silently replies "What?" I will admit it here: if you may have been among the persons of rank I shed in a negative light and you have any doubt about whether I was talking about you, the answer is probably yes. Oops, I mean yes, sir!

In the Viet Nam stories, I need to apologize to so many of you whose names I do not recall. Especially to all the crew chiefs that flew with me and without whom I would never have survived, to say nothing about being able do my job with any success. The Marine Corps concept of separation of the living quarters of officer and enlisted men was a contributor, but I also accept the primary blame of my own lack of attention and caring. I was all business when flying, with a few exceptions where grab ass was involved, and that's too bad.

This said, I do vividly remember Jim Collum, who was with me so often in his bird WB-5 on many out-of-squadron assignments, especially most of the SOG missions. He often is my mental image for many of the others of you who flew with me. Jim Collum went from PFC to Sgt while in Viet Nam because he took responsibility for all aspects of his aircraft and all those with him. Crew chiefs owned the aircraft; the pilots were only allowed to borrow them to fly the missions. They oversaw, on top of all their other responsibilities, that the pilot who was borrowing his bird was treating it properly by keeping a keen eye on it and the gauges to be sure they stayed within prescribed limits. They made sure it was properly repaired, refueled, rearmed, and that there were a few C Rations and some water tucked away so that, when we ended up flying more missions, one on top of the other, refueling and rearming wherever was closest, the crew also got "refueled." They knew all about weight and balance limits, loading gear and personnel accordingly, and kept us informed whenever we were pushing the limits so we could adjust how we flew. Many times when we were operating away from home, a maintenance issue came up. The crew chief would slide out the secret stash of tools and work his magic to make the issue go away and keep us ready to fly that next mission. When we returned to base, whatever base it was, we pilots climbed out and wandered away for a strenuous round filling out the yellow sheets and debriefing. The crew chief, on the other hand, began at least a couple of hours of hard labor. It was a pretty rare occurrence when a pilot had to refuel, rearm, clean up the cabin and cockpit or do that all time favorite—cleaning the six machine guns. I can personally attest that some crew chiefs had occasions when they also had to suffer the rigors of being a pilot, when they were flying in the left seat. Some pilots actually forced them to take the controls and learn to fly. I did sometimes hear mumbling about their other chores, but for some reason never about the stick time. Oh, we pilots sure had it rough.

Gunners are another group that seemed like a parade going through the back of the bird. You were the crew chief's responsibility and, with only one exception, did your job every time. I hope that I at least said "thank you" and "good job" as often as I should have.

During 1966 to 1967, we at the operations level had no time, no way to know and no real interest in why we were in Viet Nam. We were asked to do our job, so we did it. Most often that job was to protect and return to safety those who were suffering the consequences of doing their job. There was no philosophical discussion on the political correctness of being in Viet Nam. It was always for just one thing, taking care of those who found themselves in peril.

I have included only a few of the stories about missions as a Marine in Viet Nam, as it is not my intent to write a chronicle. I have chosen these few missions to describe, as I believe they best illustrate the emotions and the impact that the total Marine Corps and Viet Nam experience had on me. My purpose is to communicate to you how it changed me, matured me and affected the way I have led my life and interacted with my family and all those who I have met personally and professionally on this wonderful journey called life.

How I Learned to Make a Deal

Sixty years ago, when I was 6 or 7 years old, I had an experience, the implications of which I wouldn't understand until many years later. I learned this lesson from a man I had never met before, knew for less than five minutes, and have never met again.

I was raised in a small New England village of about one hundred people. A place where you knew everyone and everyone knew you. Not always a good thing for a young boy who often found fun and adventure doing things that didn't always work out exactly as planned, because, if someone saw him, his parents were sure to learn of it, maybe even before he got home.

One summer day I accompanied my mother on a visit to a neighbor's house where I could play with my friend Chris. They lived on the "main road," a Major boundary for us since the speed limit was as high as thirty-five miles per hour, much more dangerous than our village streets. As soon as we arrived, Chris and I ran off in search of adventure and our mothers went into the house for coffee and a neighborly chat. Chatting is something I have never really understood, but mothers never seemed to tire of it. It wasn't long after we began to rummage around in Chris's father's barn/garage that we came across an Indian tank. What's an Indian tank? It's a fantastic invention for use in fighting brush fires. It could be filled with water and then pumped up to high pressure. It had a hose with a nozzle attached that allowed the water to be squirted a long way. It had straps so it could be carried on your back to wherever a brush fire might be found. I do want to assure the reader that not all the brush fires in the village were started by adventurous young boys whose experiments got out of hand. Some were actually started by grown men burning brush or leaves whose plans didn't work out exactly as they had envisioned. In fact, owning an Indian tank was a pretty good indication that the owner of the tank may have had just such a situation in the past and was now better prepared in case it should ever happen again.

Well, it didn't matter to Chris and me that there were no brush fires burning at that moment; we wanted to squirt some water with what we deemed to be the best water gun we had ever had the privilege of getting our hands on. We also called upon the wisdom of our many years of experience and vetoed the idea that we could start a fire and then have a good excuse for fooling around with the Indian tank. To carry it we each put a strap on one of our shoulders and by walking right next to each other we would be able to carry it, even though it was pretty big and designed for use by an adult man. Off we went to the spigot in the front of Chris's house to load the ammo in our new weapon. After we got it full of water, we pumped it up as much as we could and gave it a few test squirts. Fantastic! It worked even better than we had imagined, shooting fifty to sixty feet and with a serious stream to boot. Okay, so what can we shoot? "I've got it," said Chris. "Let's squirt my sister. She's playing in the backyard." I immediately realized this was a good idea, so Chris and I bent down and each put a strap on one shoulder and began to stand up. Oops! When full of water the tank weighed more than either of us two small boys. We had a real dilemma. Overcoming problems was, of course, one of the strong points of adventurous boys like us. "How about we get your sister to come around over here? Then we can squirt her." We thought she was pretty stupid but probably not that stupid, and we also knew we would want to squirt some other stuff, too, so what could we do? "I know. Let's put it into your wagon and then we can pull it wherever we want to go." So Chris went to get his wagon. We then squirted all the water out of the tank, working on improving our aim and range. We got our mobile water cannon, as we now were calling it, all loaded onto the wagon, refilled with ammo, and we started off for the backyard. I guess we weren't too sneaky as our "discussion" about who was going to get to take the first shot at Chris's sister grew louder and louder. She figured out that we were up to no good and lit out for the safety of the house. Well, plan number one was out, so what was next?

At that moment we heard a car zoom by on the main road. "Let's squirt cars!" We knew we had a good idea this time, so off we went to set up our ambush position. We went back down by the garage, just behind the board fence and the hedge running along the road that gave us the cover we needed and a good vantage point from which to watch out for our targets. We now decided to take turns and Chris went first since we realized that arguing about it had not worked out so well in our first attack and, besides, there were now going to be plenty of targets.

This was working out great. We were hitting our targets fairly consistently and we could see how surprised the drivers were to have run into a small rainstorm on such a clear day. It was my turn on the gun and Chris was the lookout. Suddenly he got really excited and started yelling, "A convertible, a convertible is coming, and the top is down!" I knew luck was with me because it was my turn when this fantastic opportunity came along. I took aim and timed it just right, hitting the car from the hood ornament to the windshield and then the driver himself. I broke out into a huge grin over this great success at just the same time that the car braked to a squealing stop. Chris made a quick assessment of the situation and broke into a full dash for the high grass and the greatest distance he could make between himself and the driver of the squealing car. Still bathing in the glow of my incredible success, I was not as quick as I should have been and realized that the guy, now running towards me, was way faster than me and that I would never outrun him. So with quick thinking I climbed the fence, jumped into the small maple tree growing from the hedge, and climbed to about fifteen feet above the ground, as high as I could get in this small tree. Just as I got there, the furious, and very big, driver arrived just below me. He was swearing and yelling and was not a happy camper. He reached out, grabbed the maple and shook it. We both were very surprised when I came hurtling down and landed in the briar hedge. We both remained stunned and didn't move an inch. I quickly realized three things. One, the briars hurt; two, my nose was bleeding profusely. Neither of these was anywhere near as big a concern to me as number three, which was that I had been caught red-handed squirting cars and trouble was surely in my future. And with this realization I was overcome with distress and started to cry. In retrospect I now can understand that the driver was having very similar reactions to my own. One, he had just shook a little kid out of a tree; two, the kid was lying on the ground, crying and covered in blood. But he too was struck most strongly by his third realization—that he had been caught red-handed shaking a kid out of a tree and trouble was surely in his future. But, instead of crying, he immediately became my savior.

He picked me up in his arms, blood, stickers and all. I told him my mother was in the house right over there and off we went. He started calling, "Hello, hello," as we neared the back door. My mother quickly showed up with a look of great concern. I tried to reassure her by saying, "I'm okay." The driver looked me in the eye and then said to my mother, "I was driving by and saw him fall out of the tree down by the road. I stopped and picked him up and brought him here." I was gritting my teeth, knowing the ax was about to fall when he told her I was squirting cars, but it never came. I looked up at him and realized we had just made a deal. He wasn't going to say anything about squirting cars, so you can bet I wasn't going say anything about shaking trees. We were in full accord, and both understood the bargain completely. My mother thanked him, he and I shook hands, and he left. I got cleaned up and went back out to play. and to disassemble our mobile water cannon and return the Indian tank to its original storage place before any questions were raised. He and I had both had a good day, and we both owed the other for it. Debt incurred, debt paid.

The lesson here is straightforward. When you need something from people, do not waste your time trying to figure out how to get it away from them. Instead, look for something that they need and then figure out how to give it to them. That's the true art of the deal.

How I Became a Marine

It was June, 47 years ago in 1963 when I woke up to the realization that things weren't working out so well. I had been in college for two years, hadn't flunked out yet, but the handwriting was on the wall. I was having a lot of fun, partying every chance I had, and there were a lot of parties. The problem was that there were also classes and studying which were not getting the attention they needed and deserved.

I needed "straightening out." I had heard that phrase a lot while growing up. "You'd better straighten up, young man." "Straighten up and fly right." "Go down the straight and narrow path." Yup, that's what I needed. I'd get back to studying after I got "straightened out."

So how do you get straightened out? I knew—I'd go into the military. The military straightened people out. Everybody who had been in the military seemed pretty on track to me. Judges sometimes let people avoid jail if they went into the military. So the decision was made.

In those days the military recruiters had their offices in the basement of the post office. So I drove home from college and went directly there. The first office was the Army. The recruiter invited me right in, asked some questions, gave me a quick test, and explained that he had a great deal for me. If I signed up for just two years, I could pick any base around the world at which to serve my enlistment. I could go to Germany, Japan, and other great places. He had brochures explaining how nice each place was. Not bad, I said, I'll get back to you. The next office was the Air Force. There's lots of glamour and prestige in the Air Force. It was the same routine: a little chat, a short test, and this recruiter, too, had a deal for me. If you sign up for three years, you can pick any of these specialty schools—radio technician, jet mechanic, radar technician, and more. Not bad, I said, I'll get back to you. It was the same routine with the Navy, but this recruiter's deal was even better. I could pick both the school and the base I wanted. Not bad, I said, I'll get back to you.

There was one office left but it was now after five and it was closed. So off I went—to party, of course. The next morning I showed up at the post office again. The Marine recruiter was there so I went right in. I knew the routine now. I had the material and the offers from the other services so I was ready to deal. There was no chit-chat or tests, I started right in. He listened quietly while I told him about the Army deal, the Air Force deal and the Navy deal. I asked him what kind of deal he had for me. He slowly leaned across his desk until his face was only about three inches from mine and said, "We don't have deals in the Marine Corps. We will tell you what we need you to do and you will do it. If you're any good, the Marine Corps will be good to you." He then leaned back in his chair and didn't say anything else.

Well, you can be sure I was taken aback. This was certainly not what I had expected. I sputtered and hemmed and hawed as I backed out of there and fled to the street. I needed to think about this and make a choice. What would be my best deal?

For the rest of the day I balanced different schools and different bases, but I couldn't get the picture of that Marine out of my head. I kept flashing back to what he had said. When I eventually got back to the reason I was doing this in the first place, I remembered it was to get "straightened out." When I focused on that objective, I quickly realized there was only one choice.

That Marine was the most "straightened out" person I had ever met. So why go halfway? I went back the next day and signed up. Two weeks later, at about eleven o'clock at night, I was aboard a bus that had picked up a group of us from the train station in Beaufort, South Carolina and was now arriving, after a short ride, at Marine Recruit Depot, Parris Island. A 6'6" 250 lb Marine stepped aboard and announced to us "Your mother isn't here and from this minute on your ass belongs to me." At that point I was way less than sure about the wisdom of my choice.

But, not too many weeks or days from that point, I slowly became sure that I had made the right choice. And after all these many years, I grow firmer in my understanding of how much the Marine Corps has meant in my life. I can't explain it, but we Marines know. It is why we can look each other in the eye and say *Semper Fi*. We don't need to say any more, because we know and respect what we did for the Corps and, even more importantly, what the Corps did for us. Did I get "straightened out?" Let's you and I talk sometime and then you can decide.

Are you wondering about the deal I got from the Marines, who made me no promises, and always told me what they wanted me to do, whenever they needed me to do it? Pretty much, but not always, as you will read, I gave them what they asked from me, and often more. Well, I ended up commissioned as a Captain; they made me a Marine Cadet (MARCAD) and sent me to flight school; they let me land on an aircraft carrier and sent me to war, where I was able to help save more people on many a single day than most people ever have a chance to help in a lifetime. I gave the Marine Corps my best and they did the same for me, again and again and again. Once a Marine, always a Marine and you can bet on it.

From Scumbag to Marine

B oot camp in the Marine Corps is a different experience for everyone. We all did many of the same activities, felt the same emotions, and learned how to be better then we thought we could be. But I also had fate touching me in so many ways. It would steer me to places over the next five years that were far, far beyond the realm of what I could conceive and would lead me to find joy doing things, going places, meeting people, and living life to the max.

You will never be happier than when you are functioning at your fullest. The Marine Corps asked me to do things that pushed me, not just to the limits, but also past them. It started in small ways. Only looking back after so much time has passed can I see how the experiences built slowly, one upon the other, to help me meet the challenges I would be handed. I didn't look for opportunities; in fact, most often I didn't see them as opportunities at all, but that's what they were. When you are in boot camp you don't have the right of choice about what you will do, how you will do it or when you will do it.

I did get one opportunity to make a choice on my first day on Parris Island, while I was still in the reception building. The sergeant told us to go to the second deck (i.e., the second floor—just one of the hundreds of things we were going to learn that we had been referring to incorrectly all our lives), to urinate in the first or the second urinal, and not to wash our hands or touch anything else in his perfectly spit and polished head (not "bathroom;" this was the second new word). I, of course, while not having been particularly worried about this point of hygiene before, decided to use what I had in the past classified as a brain to determine that I must have heard him incorrectly. The Marine Corps would always teach us to use proper sanitation procedures such as washing after urinating, so I went to the sink when I was done, turned on the water, and almost instantly felt a very large finger enter my right ear and proceed through my head, very effectively cleaning the dirt out of both the right and the left ears at the same time. It was amazing how much more clearly I was able to hear every word now, as I was being yelled at from a face that was about one millimeter from mine, explaining to me that what he had said was what he had meant. Many, including myself at the time, would not see this as an opportunity, but it was. It was the opportunity to realize that when the Marine Corps wanted me to think, they would provide me with ample warning. This opportunity helped me avoid a lot of problems during the ensuing weeks.

Boot Camp

You can learn about Marine Corps boot camp from any marine so I won't get into that experience, except the parts about being selected for flight school. My whole concept of the Marines was landing on the beaches and fighting eyeball to eyeball just like the World War II movies. I had never heard of the famous Colonel Pappy Boyington and his Black Sheep squadron and their incredible feats in the Pacific in the Second World War, and the fact that Marines could be pilots never even crossed my mind. But this was the start of "being in the right place at the right time" that made the next five years the great experience it would be.

As part of the program at Parris Island we were all tested for this, that and the other thing. This let our superiors get some feel for who could be a mechanic, an office clerk, a radar technician, or any of the thousands of things that Marines do to get the job done. A week or so after these basic tests had been completed for my platoon, I was told to report to the building where we had previously taken the tests. It was the first time I was actually out of the sight or direct control of a drill instructor. There were some other recruits there as well and we took more tests and then were ordered back to our barracks. After a few days it happened again. Remember that we did not ask questions. If there was something they wanted us to know, they would tell us. This battery of tests gave me some clues, however, that this had something to do with airplanes. The tests contained spatial relations questions that used pictures of planes and gauges. Also, the tests had titles related to qualifying for pilot training.

It was soon after these tests that I began to get some special extra attention. If you were thinking this was a good thing, you would be very wrong. Boot camp platoons have three drill instructors (DIs) and each plays a different role. I learned later that they actually change the role they play with different platoons. There is the head drill instructor, who plays tough but fair, the next, who is nice and seems to actually understand that it is hard work being on Parris Island, and then the last, who is tough, mean, nasty, unforgiving, and generally there to make your life as miserable as possible. The extra attention I received was from—you guessed it—the mean one. He would step on my boots, holding on to the front of my shirt, pulling himself up so that his nose was almost touching mine and scream, "You may think you're smart enough to become an officer and fly planes, Boden, but that doesn't mean a damn thing because, unless you get an okay from me, it will never happen. When you do stuff as stupid as you do, you can bet I would never want you to be an officer or to fly a plane in my Marine Corps, so you can just forget it." I would get these little pecks on the cheek two or three times a day.

One day I was told to report to the parade ground. There was a car waiting there for me, and the driver told me to get in and off we went. Not only was I away from the DIs, but the driver was friendly and chatting away as if I was a real person. He told me we were on our way to the

Marine Corps Air Station (MCAS) in Beaufort, South Carolina, where I was going to get a flight physical. The day spent at Beaufort was like a vacation. I was treated like a human being the whole time. When I went to the mess hall, I found it was huge and had all kinds of different food options. People helped me out and sat with me and we leisurely chatted while we ate. It reminded me that there would be a real world out there after boot camp was over.

After thirteen weeks I finally reached graduation day and was promoted to PFC (Private First Class E-2), which meant I was in the top ten percent of the platoon in spite of all the flak I seemed to get day in and day out. I also learned I was not going to leave for infantry training school at Camp Geiger in North Carolina with the rest of the platoon. I would be staying on at Parris Island for a week or ten days waiting for processing, as I had been selected to be a Marine Cadet (MARCAD). This meant I had to sign agreements to serve for three years after graduating from flight school and becoming commissioned as a second lieutenant. I would go on to Camp Geiger as soon as all of the paperwork was done and approved. I was assigned, along with another new graduate who was also waiting for his MARCAD paperwork, to supervise the Casual Platoon. The Casual Platoon was a collection of misfits, bed-wetters, PT (physical fitness) failures, and even a guy who had tried to stab his drill instructor. They were the recruits that even the Marine Corps couldn't straighten out and soon would be mustered out of the Corps. My co-supervisor was John Longdin, and this was the start of a long friendship. You will see him again in my stories since we came back together again on and off through our service and beyond. Supervising this gang of about fifty was not hard work. We needed to get them up, washed, dressed, and marched to the mess hall each morning. During the day we could read and relax while we watched the group out of the corner of our eyes. After we got them back from supper, we were free to walk around and investigate the base for a couple of hours.

It was during one those excursions that I came across my drill instructor, the mean and nasty one. He was marching a brand new platoon across the parade ground and, as we neared each other, he halted the platoon and, while they were standing there, he came over and reached out to shake my hand. I couldn't believe it. We stayed there and talked for over fifteen minutes. He was a great guy. He told me I had done really well and he was proud that I was selected for flight school. He was sure I would do well and he would be proud to serve under me. It was then that I realized just how hard drill instructors have it, always having to keep up the pressure to instill in us the same sense of pride they have in both themselves and the Marine Corps.

I went on to Camp Geiger and then home for boot leave. I was home and very different from the kid who had left five months before to get "straightened out." The job wasn't done yet, but progress had been made.

MARCAD

After my visit home I arrived at Naval Air Station (NAS) Pensacola, Florida with my sea bag and orders in hand and absolutely no idea of what was in store. It was November 20, 1963, a few days before my actual report date, but I wanted to save the leave time. I was logged in and then assigned to a large room on the second floor with about twenty bunks in it, all empty. I was the only one there. I was told to get dressed in my utilities (working clothes), and then it began. The cadet officers, a role that all cadets filled during their last week before graduating from the four months of ground school, began the hazing. I was given a tooth brush and told to start cleaning the head. With the exception of meals and sleeping, I continued to clean every inch of the whole area and, when done, I started over. No one else showed up and, on the third day of scrubbing toilets and baseboards with a toothbrush, the cadet officers pulled what I thought was a harassment trick that went far beyond the pale. They told me the president had been shot. Yeah, sure! I was still made to keep on scrubbing that day and the next. When they took me off to church on Sunday, I learned it was true. Everyone can remember where they were when Kennedy was assassinated and the feelings it caused, except someone who was stuck away in what had to have been one of the very few places that had no TV, with no one to commiserate with while endlessly grieving the tragedy and who was forced to keep on cleaning with the toothbrush. We then went to church the following day for the memorial service, then to church again on Thursday for Thanksgiving. I was really beginning to wonder about this outfit. You can also be sure that my attitude about pompous military jerks was now set in stone and would continue to worsen for the next five years.

Finally a class of eight MARCADs and about twice as many NAVCADs (Navy version of MARCADs) was formed, and ground school began. We did our academics along with the commissioned officers who were also in Pensacola for flight school. In fact it was then I realized how easy life was for the officers who were going to ground school with us compared to that of a cadet. I swore I would never let a piece of paper called a degree keep me separated from, or deny me access to, opportunities or privileges offered to people who were no better than I except for that diploma.

After about two months I was hospitalized, having fainted during a bout with the flu while I was using the head. I had hit a water faucet and seriously cut my eye. I was in the hospital about two weeks. I had to cheat on the eye exam as I was still seeing double when they discharged me, but I was not going to get washed out of the program for some temporary problem like seeing double. My vision was soon fine and I returned to my normal 40/20—yes, twice what is average. You will learn more later, along with my adventures racing the Navy yawls, why that caused me to graduate a month or more after my original 44-1963 class, which had moved the few miles to Saufley Field and begun to actually fly.

My attitude about spit and polish, folding socks and underwear 4" by 4" and other activities of this type led me to be a near record holder for demerits. Demerits were marched off on the parade ground, often referred to as the "grinder," during any period classified as free time, and there was not much of that. This assured that, whatever class I was attached to, I always held the honor of having the most demerits and the lowest grades in Military Science, one of the three areas we were graded in. Thank God for Physical Fitness and Academics or I would have been back in grunt land for sure.

During the last week of ground school, cadet officer week, we were assigned a rank from Colonel down to second lieutenant based on the combined total of our grades in the three disciplines. That week I had the unique distinction of winning the award for being first in the class in Academics, first in the class for Physical Fitness and then being made a second lieutenant when all three scores were combined. Love that spit and polish crap, the bane of my existence.

MARCAD Boden

MARCAD Longdin

More information and photos at
www.klondikeplayboy.com

High and Fast

I survived ground school after a couple of extra months and was on my way to Basic Flight Training at Saufley Field to actually start flying. Another advantage of moving on, almost as good as flying, was that the harassment phase was now over. We were still very much in the Marine Corps so it was not as if it was okay to slack off; we still needed to polish and shine, but it wasn't a constant war with some over-zealous cadet officer.

This was real work but we all tore right in to learn everything we could about the T-34 trainer plane. Finally, our assigned instructor took us on our first familiarization (Fam-1) hop. It was a ball. The first thing he tried to do was to see if we would get airsick, so he did every maneuver in the book, including aerobatic maneuvers which put both positive and negative G forces on us and, of course, also on our stomachs. For most of us it was the best ride we had ever had. One sea story the instructor told was about a Fam-1 during which his student, referred to with the universal term "stud," vomited when they were inverted. The vomit was sitting on the inside of the canopy just waiting for him to roll back to normal flight when gravity would get it down. Since the T-34 could only stay inverted for 30 seconds at a time, this was a real dilemma. While yelling and screaming at this low life he had in the front seat, he pushed the nose down, really up when inverted, so the puddle flowed over, under when inverted, his stud and snap rolled back to normal level flight. Of course this caused the offending blob to return to the close proximity of its source. The instructor slid open his canopy so he could get some fresh air and returned to base. I do not know if the student made it through the program, but he would not have been the first or the last to wash out on airsickness. After 12 or 13 hours of dual training time I made my first solo flight. That is followed by a tie cutting ceremony at the next Friday night happy hour. The instructors would collect the ends of the ties from their soloed students like the scalps collected by Plains Indians. I can hear their wives a few years later asking them when they were going to throw out that stupid box of brown rags. I advanced through the basic program, again with delays due to sailing and one experience I will mention later, and I was on to Whiting Field, about 25 miles northeast of Pensacola with the T-28s.

The Navy T-28 was a real plane. It went like a bat out of hell, climbed, pulled Gs, and could be hauled around like a bucking bronco for aerobatics and dogfights. She had enough power to launch herself off the carrier deck without a catapult. It was one hell of a lot of fun to fly.

It was in the T-28 that I learned the importance of flying with precision, being smooth, and always thinking ahead to what is going to happen and what might happen if something goes wrong. Flying aerobatics with the plane never leaving its compass heading as you do roll after roll and feeling the turbulence left in the spot you started the maneuver, called your spoiled air, as you arrive at the bottom of a loop on heading and altitude, is a very satisfying experience. Flying on instruments taught us a level of concentration that is hard to match.

One of the highlights was, of course, becoming a Tailhooker. You could claim this title after the process of approaching the aircraft carrier a first time and being waved off to go around, then making your touch and go landing with your hook up and stowed, and then being fully arrested with your hook having grabbed the wire and brought you to the quickest stop you have ever experienced. And then doing it again five more times.

Two weeks before I qualified as a Tailhooker on the *USS Lexington*, they had a new experience with a T-28 landing. For the first, and the last, time they were able to log a T-28 making a full stop landing on their deck without the use of arresting gear. A stud made his initial approach and was waved off. He then began his next approach for a touch and go with his hook properly up and stowed, but, instead of throwing on full power to take back off, he jumped on the brakes and went screeching down to the right of the angle deck, with smoke coming from the brakes, and came to a halt with his nose gear about one foot from the bow round down, or one foot away from falling overboard and being then run over by the ship. As if this were not enough to cause everyone to have conniptions, his next move would be.

When they got to him, they were frantically signaling him to shut down the engine. He didn't want to do anything else wrong after this last screw-up so, to the deck crew's utter disbelief, and as he sat inches from falling to his death, he began the "proper" shut down procedure, which was to run the engine up to 1,200 RPM for thirty seconds to purge the oil and then to shut off the magnetos. They finally got him out of the cockpit, the plane secured, and the heart rates of all the witnesses back to somewhere near normal. He was discharged for the reason that he had "No apparent fear of death."

Another carrier qualification story worth telling is about the T-28 that made an arrested landing on the *USS Lexington* that caused the deck crew to think it had landed on its own, since they could not see a pilot. Upon leaping up onto the wing and looking into the cockpit they saw a huge orange blob crammed on the floor and under the instrument panel. It was pretty obvious that this orange blob was a pilot who had forgotten to lock his seatbelt. The blob managed to get himself back into his seat, recover his wits, take off and do the rest of his landings, with the harness locked, of course.

I have recently learned, forty-five years later, that a friend and fellow UH-1E pilot admitted that the same thing had happened to him. But he swears that the orange blob I heard about could not have been him because he was so fast getting back into his seat that the deck crew never knew what had happened. The only difference in the stories was his ability to make a quick recovery. Or, from my point of view, maybe he was concentrating so hard on getting back into his seat that he never saw the swabby peering through his canopy and watching him. Or possibly the swabby was laughing so hard he fell off the wing before my friend could look up and see him.

I also think the reason it took him this long to overcome the embarrassment and finally admit the story is that he has reached a point in his life where, compared to his other screw-ups, this one no longer seems so bad.

I do have to admit I am quite sure he wasn't the only one to be shot out of his seat when the wire jerked him to a stop. My memory, of course, is way too blurred to remember details like unlocking one's harness to touch the items on the checklist, which is his explanation why his was unlocked. I am not so sure that unlocking the harness for any reason was a good idea except for things like getting a smoke out of the ankle pocket of your flight suit or some other very serious situation like that.

Another great part of our training in the T-28 was formation flying, flying while snuggled up to a plane in front and to the side of you with two more snuggled up to you the same way. It demanded precision control and intense attention to detail in every action you took.

One of the last formation flights in this part of the program was to solo in a four plane formation cross country flight with an instructor following in a fifth plane. Our formation cross-country flight was to Beaufort MCAS, where I had my one day vacation from Parris Island. We were taking off after having lunch to head back to Whiting. I was number two in the flight so was cleared for takeoff after number one was airborne and had started his turn. I was in the process of joining up with him and had popped the speed brake and pulled back the throttle to slow and match his speed. As soon as I started to add power back, the motor started backfiring and backfiring forcefully enough to make the engine cowl expand as if it was going to fly off. I pulled away from the leader and tried a couple more times to put power back, with the same result. I switched back to the tower frequency and declared an emergency. I had a pilot's best friends—altitude and air speed—and would have no trouble coming downwind and then turning for a landing on the runway I had just taken off from. It seemed like less than thirty seconds when the standby Search and Rescue (SAR) H-34 safety crew was on the air with me, encouraging me and keeping me cool and relaxed. Everything was going like clockwork when I heard the instructor flying the fifth chase plane come up on the tower frequency and ask, "I am missing one of my chicks. Do you know where he is?" "Yes," they responded, "he is downwind for runway nine to make an emergency landing since he cannot add power." The helicopter came up then to say that they were airborne and had me in sight and that all looked good. The landing went great. I landed about six feet short in the gravel, which was no problem. I rolled out, turned off the runway onto a taxiway and shut down. The engine had never quit; it just wouldn't take power. We left that plane there and I took the front seat of the instructor's plane. We took off and joined up with the flight that had been waiting for us and went home. This was not my first emergency landing or the first time that I landed six feet short of the runway. I will tell that story a little later.

8-4-64

Tie Cutting

CADET JOHN B. BODEN

... Takes Solo Flight

Marine Aviation Cadet John B. Boden, Jr., son of Mr. and Mrs. John B. Boden, Sr., o Route 1, Foot Hills Road, Dur ham took a giant stride towar winning his coveted "Wings o Gold" at Pensacola, Fla., re cently when he flew his first sol flight in the "Mentor" trainer.

During primary flight train ing, he is receiving academic training in communications, navigation, engineering, ath letics, aerology and civil air regulations.

Upon completion of this in struction, he will advance to another stage of aviation train ing at another field, either in Pensacola or Meridian, Miss.

Solo Clipping

Solo Photo Navy

More information and photos at
www.klondikeplayboy.com

Low and Slow

Upon graduation from fixed wing, advanced training and more than a year into the program, it was time to go our separate ways—jets, multi-engine planes or helicopters. We had some choice, but jets was the choice for almost all of us since it was seen as what real men did—go fast and fly high. Some were actually thinking ahead to a future in aviation and wanted to go multi-engine in preparation for a career in the airlines. There were other factors in the wind, which we were not aware of, that meant that a large majority of us Marines were assigned to helicopters. I was not unhappy since I had no strong preference and would not be leaving Whiting Field and the Pensacola area so I could continue my sailing activities with all the attendant fun that involved.

We started with the Bell H-13 trainer. It was a plastic bubble with some pipes welded together to keep the tail rotor on. One thing was soon very apparent: keeping one of those things under control took a hell of a lot of skill. Fixed wing planes, by their nature, want to fly and, if not over-controlled by a pilot, do reasonably well on their own. A helicopter is exactly the opposite. It will fly only with a pilot wrestling it under control with sheer will, attitude and acquired skill. The newest versions made today are only easier to fly because the equipment, computers, stabilizers, etc., do a lot of the wrestling for the pilots, leaving them to conduct themselves more like fixed wing pilots.

I finally got the hang of it, even of the practice emergency procedure called a forty and forty. This was to cut the power when you were at forty feet and forty knots and auto-rotate to a landing. I think this was something that Bell devised to increase sales, and it worked. A fair number of the craft got turned into spare parts when the maneuver wasn't executed perfectly. Maybe "executed" was not the best word to use here. It was also a good snake killer. While practicing hovering in the grass fields set aside for this, I often would see snakes trying to get away from the huge raptor that was surely there to eat them. Chasing them around and then bouncing the skid on them was actually a big help in building skill, to say nothing of adding to the fun.

It was then on to the H-34, where we learned what a big, strong workhorse bird could do. As soon as we learned to control her, we were lifting cargo, using the hoist for rescues, and learning that a helicopter on instruments was another whole world in the difficulty department.

The day finally came in July 1965, two years and two months after joining the Marine Corps; my training was complete and I got my wings and my commission as a second lieutenant. This was toasted at a "wetting down," the ceremony celebrating promotion. There was, of course, a special ceremony for getting your wings which involved drinking an "After Burner". It was in a Tom Collins glass, with no ice, and consisted of a shot of all the bar's well drinks topped off with Crème de Menthe, which made it a rather unappealing green color. Your new wings were dropped into the glass and you were to catch them in your teeth as you downed the drink in one big gulp. Not that difficult and, if you had any sense, you went to the head and did then what you would soon be doing later if you hadn't.

After I came back from Viet Nam and was an instructor pilot back at the New River Marine Air Station in Jacksonville, North Carolina, we heard a story about a clown who had swallowed his wings while drinking his After Burner. It sounded like a good story but hard to believe until a few days later when a new stud showed up, bragging about swallowing his wings and saying he had the x-rays to prove it. The bragging was pretty short-lived when he saw how hard we all laughed at him and let him know that we agreed there was probably no damage as he still had plenty of asshole left.

Finding the Zone

H ave you ever been in a situation where time slows down, vision is crystal clear, every noise is sharp and distinct, and your mind works like a computer? Athletes often refer to it as "being in the zone." They hit the home run, catch the impossible pass, leap higher than any other person because they have concentrated, trained and practiced to attain levels of performance which only a very few can even dream about.

This experience is not reserved for athletes, musicians, surgeons, and the many others who have made the effort to achieve a goal and, in the process, been in the zone. Often we everyday people have something happen to us that suddenly puts us in the zone. Time slows, our minds sharpen, we move instinctively, and we don't even realize we are there until it is all over: for example, the person who races into a burning building and saves someone or the person who pulls a drowning swimmer from the surf.

I cannot speak for how others viewed their experiences when they looked back on them, but I can tell you my thoughts about something that happened to me. I was not a hero, I didn't save anyone, and no one else was even there. I was at Pensacola Naval Air Station in Florida. It was 1964, when I was twenty two years old and in flight school. I had about fifteen or sixteen hours of flight time in the primary trainer T-34 and was on my third solo flight. If you can remember the first time you drove a car by yourself, you will be able to relate to how I was feeling. I was doing okay, and everything was working out since I concentrated on every detail. I was not afraid, but I surely was not confident either.

I had done about six touch-and-go landings at an outlying field and was practicing turns at about four thousand feet when suddenly the engine stopped. Instantly an amazing thing happened. I went into the zone. All the training, all the practice emergencies when the instructor pulled back the power and declared there was an engine failure kicked in. I immediately began all the procedures—check the fuel, check the gauges, switch tanks, set the mixture, set the throttle, try for a restart, look for a place to land, switch to guard channel, call your emergency, and try it all again. Everything went smoothly, except for one detail—the engine did not restart. So after three tries there was now only one goal. Get back on the ground in one piece. I had two friends with me—air speed and altitude. I located the field where I had been doing the landings, set my course, made my plan, radioed my intentions, and flew the plane. There was no sweat, no worry, no fear, and no thought of it not working out.

The result was not perfect; I landed about six feet short of the asphalt on the gravel, which of course was no problem. I rolled out on the runway to where the crash truck, that stands duty at every outlying field when flight training is in progress, was parked, then braked and climbed out of the plane. I learned the crash crew had never gotten the word about my emergency because they told me I could not do a full stop landing there. Everything felt perfectly normal to me, as if this were just a regular day—no rush, no relief, and no exhilaration. They sent out a plane and picked me up, and that was that.

It was not until years later that I understood what happened that day, and it is now remembered as one of my life's peaks. A time when I exceeded myself, accomplishing more than I had thought I was capable of doing. I had been "in the zone" and that was a very good feeling.

Thank you, Life. You were very good to me that day.

The Skipper

This story is a perfect example to show that being in the right place at the right time is the greatest factor in getting the opportunities of a lifetime. It was a warm Sunday afternoon in the spring of 1964. After eating lunch at the mess hall, I was walking around near the docks where the aircraft carrier *USS Lexington* was tied up. I was well into my basic ground school training as a Marine Cadet. Being able to take a walk occurred only rarely—when I had no demerits to be marched off on the parade ground. I was in my uniform, as civilian clothes were not allowed. I was watching the sea gulls doing aerobatics using the wind currents from the seaplane hangar roofs. They would come speeding right at the curving section of the roof, catch the up draft, and do aerobatic maneuvers like loops and Imulmanns. I wonder if aviators taught these moves to the gulls or if the gulls taught them to the aviators? As I continued walking and sticking my nose into every area around the docks, I suddenly saw a mast sticking up out of a large wet slip and a bunch of people on the seawall getting ready to board and go sailing. I went over to check it out and was amazed to see beer, girls, guitars, food and I immediately knew this was a party in the making. I hadn't even thought about a party in a long time, having been in the clutches of a ruthless dictatorship that was running the MARCAD ground training. There may have been some leeway in this

49

matter for some cadets, but as one who graduated last in his class in the category of military science (polishing shoes, shining brass, folding underwear, and the other related duties that I was never too enthusiastic about), I spent a lot of my "free" time paying for my sins by marching off my near record number of demerits. It was a good thing I could read, add, subtract, and multiply and swim, run, jump and do push-ups well enough to keep from being washed out and sent back to grunt land.

I asked, "What's the story here?" and got the best possible reply, "If you want to come along, take off those shoes and come aboard." This was the start of a lot of very good times and one very wild adventure. I had been sailing, mostly in small boats, since I was a boy living on the banks of the Connecticut River. But that made me an expert compared to all but a few of those aboard this boat. The three or four people who had been involved in getting the Naval Academy to give this boat, renamed *Tailwind*, to the flight school were working hard to get more people involved in sailing.

Tailwind was the oldest of the Academy's wooden boats, when they got their first new fiberglass boats as a replacement for their fleet in Annapolis. I believe her former name was *Intrepid*. We also got another one a few months later, which I believe was named *Alert* and renamed *Challenger*. They were 44' Luders—yawls designed and built for the Academy from 1939 to 1943. They were beautiful boats and performed well yet were forgiving when those sailing her made mistakes, which we often did.

This was the best afternoon I had had in a long, long time. There was beer, singing, girls, and the joy of helping to harness nature's natural forces and making a boat do your bidding. When the skipper realized I knew the pointy end from the square end he was anxious to see that I continued to come back. He got all my information, including my unit. From that point on it seemed that, if they were going sailing, I got a message that I was to be excused from whatever I was doing and to report to the docks in "appropriate uniform" at the specified time. Since most of the sailing was on weekends and evenings and on some Thursday afternoons in never ending duels with a local boat named *Niki*, I didn't miss much of what I needed to be learning, but it really cut into the time reserved for marching off demerits. In fact, through some miracle, the time I spent sailing was credited against demerits after I mentioned the issue one day to the skipper that was doing so much to keep me involved in the sailing program. I knew I was in heaven then.

As summer approached, the weekend racing series sponsored by the Pensacola Yacht Club got underway. *Alert* had arrived by this time so now there were two full crews needed. This was all part of being in the right place at the right time since there was, of course, a natural rivalry between the two boats at the same time that there was a shortage of qualified crew. Soon I was a foredeck captain, running the drills for sail replacements and getting the spinnaker up and down. No easy task on a boat this size. I went back and forth between the two boats because I was assigned depending on where I was needed. As a Cadet I held a rank below almost everyone on the boats except other Cadets. Soon this was causing a small dilemma as Navy Lieutenants and Commanders were in the crew, but most didn't have the skills needed to give directions while we were aboard. This began the club designations of Foredeck Captain, Watch Captain, Bay Skipper, Race Skipper, and Off Shore Race Skipper. These designations reset the chain of command while we were aboard, and it caused some grumbling at the top that a twenty-one year old kid was in charge. But it was nothing short of glee for me, and I had to be careful while we were aboard and I was the skipper not to let a stupid grin give away my pleasure at correcting someone of rank, who on shore would be demanding that it all be "yes, sir", "no, sir." Soon it was not an issue because all of us steadily gained skill and became part of tight-knit teams with mutual respect for each other. For me it was the first time I was a skipper, and it meant a lot then and it still does now. I will take the title of skipper any time and proudly work my butt off to deserve it.

Soon I was a bay skipper and then a race skipper. I was able to take the boats with my own crew almost any time, since there were only four skippers during most of the time I was there. I was a race skipper for about a third of the formal races. But, of course, anytime there was more than one boat in the bay, there was a race; thus it has always been and shall always be when two boats under sail are in sight of each other.

There were a few challenges to sailing these boats that most did not have to deal with, the biggest being that they had no motors. This feature was surely what separated the men from the boys when it came to boat handling. As I mentioned, the boats were docked on the wall of a large wet slip about 125 feet wide and 400 feet long. There were a few times when a stiff breeze right out of the bay required us to get a tow out. Once, when we were completely becalmed out in the bay, the chief in charge of the small boats realized that, since we weren't home and it was getting dark, perhaps we needed a little help and came out and towed us home.

To get underway we would push off the wall, back the mizzen, play with the jib and do whatever we could to get out into the bay. It was often not pretty, but it usually worked. Getting in was another story. In case you do not know the main purpose of an engine in a sailboat, it is to stop your forward motion or to back up. Two maneuvers that a sailboat is really poor at. To overcome this challenge we had a sea anchor (a canvas cone with a line that we could throw over the stern) to help stop our forward motion and good crew to back sails. If we came in too fast, we would make the 180 degree turn in the 125 feet of space we had available and the boat would shoot right past our berth and force us to get back out into the bay and try again. If we were going too slowly, the boat wouldn't get all the way around and would put her bow into the seawall, often with a loud crunching noise. With a little practice and a crew that had done the maneuver before, it went surprisingly well most of the time. We used to take the boats into the Pensacola Yacht Club docks after the races to enjoy the party and award ceremonies. I don't think a lot of the members realized we were coming onto their docks without a motor the first couple of times we did it since there would have been a lot more commotion on their part, worrying that we would smash their docks or one of their boats while getting in or getting out. We never did, at least that I knew about.

It was early in 1965 when plans were getting started for the two Navy boats to join in a race that March from Pensacola to St Petersburg. It was to be a pre-race before the start of the SORC (Southern Ocean Racing Circuit) and the longest race for everyone who entered. This was going to be a big step for us since it was going to be our first off-shore experience. We got the crews set for each of the two boats and began to practice in earnest. It made a big difference to our capabilities to work with the same crew and form a good team that was able to really get the most from the boats. I was assigned the role of navigator and also watch captain along with a British Lt. Commander on exchange named Peter Beck, who had the other watch. A Navy lieutenant Bill Griffin was the captain. He was a good guy and was a big help in getting me my ratings that brought me the responsibility and use of these two great boats.

We had about a month to get everything ready and, since we were all still doing our everyday duties, we worked at it mostly during weekends and evenings. As it got down to the last week, two of our crew members announced they were not going to be able to go. This led to some scrambling around that turned out very well in the end. There was a second lieutenant, a flight student who had very little experience but who had been pestering us to let him go on this race. He had even volunteered to be the cook. He was ecstatic when he got the word he could come. I shanghaied the last member, John Longdin, a very good friend of mine whom I had met in Parris Island while we were waiting for our orders for flight school. He had gone sailing with us a couple of times but was more enthusiastic about the parties on the boat than the actual sailing. You will see later in the story that these two, especially John, delivered when the chips were down.

Provisioning was handled in typical Navy fashion. A requisition for food for ten men for ten days was sent to the mystery people who always delivered whatever was needed for the boats and here would come more food than we could get on board. So that was not an issue. There was, however, a critical item that could not be supplied by this source. BEER!

The two yawls were not US Navy vessels so did not come under the no alcohol rule, thank God. So, to fix this lack, we took up a collection from the crew and went to find where we could buy the most beer for the least money. It turned out that Budweiser was just launching a new brand called Busch. It was in the new-fangled cans called pop-tops which didn't need an opener. What a great idea that was. To get this new brand with the new can on the market, they had a very low introductory price and so we were able to buy twenty cases for each boat. I don't know how we thought we would really drink that much, but we were sure that more was better than less. We stored the beer in the bilges to keep the weight low. There will be more to the story about the beer as this saga unfolds.

The big day finally arrived and both boats left the dock with our well-wishers waving to us from the deck of the *USS Lexington*, which was open for visitors that day to watch the start of the race. The boats gathered and began to jockey for position at the starting line, which was inside the bay. Boom; off went the starting gun and we were underway, headed for what we thought would be about a two day run to cover the 300 miles to St. Petersburg. As we came out of the inlet into the Gulf of Mexico, we found winds in the range of twenty to twenty-five knots from the northeast, which seemed to bring up the thrill as we reduced sail to the small jib, took two reefs to reduce the main, and furled the mizzen.

A Major weakness in our crew preparation soon began to rear its ugly head. The bay sailors were getting seasick and were dropping like flies. You may notice in the photo our sail rig and that there are only four of us on deck when the plane went over to take the picture, and it was not even rough yet. The four consisted of Peter Beck, John Longdin, the fellow that had so little experience but begged to come along to be the cook and myself at the wheel. This meant that Peter and I were the only crew members with knowledge and experience who were not below in their bunks vomiting all over themselves and wishing they would die; a wish they came perilously close to fulfilling.

The seas and the wind continued to build and *Tailwind* was starting to moan and groan, telling us about the pain in her aging skin, bones and tendons. There was not going to be any need for a cook, and he was doing more poorly by the hour so we sent him below with the others. I do not want to say that the three of us left on deck were not also suffering from seasickness, but we weren't vomiting and we were operational. Each time I went below to record our dead reckoning position, it had to be a two-trip process. Down once to get the chart and gear out of the dry drawer and set up, and then back up on deck to clear the vertigo; then down a second time to make the plot and restore the gear, and back up as fast as possible.

Navigation in 1965 did not consist of looking at your GPS chart plotter and knowing exactly where you were every minute. We had a compass and a knot meter. While we were still in sight of land I could triangulate from marks on the shore, but that soon ended and the cloud cover and then the darkness left only one way to work. Every 30 minutes the helmsman would write down his best guess of the average course he had steered and the average speed over the water. Using these numbers and my best estimate of the speed and direction of the currents and our leeway, I would plot my estimate of our positions on the chart with the time. I would make these plots at least every four hours, using each of the helmsman's estimates since the last recording.

By the middle of the first night we were no longer trying to keep a heading to St. Petersburg. We had all the sail off the boat and were running under bare poles, with only one objective—to keep the boat with the seas on our port quarter. The temperature had dropped and dropped and we couldn't stop shivering. We were trying to avoid four things from happening: a wave coming directly up our stern and pooping us; a wave coming directly on our beam and rolling us over; falling off the wave forward and running the bow under water; and, finally, broaching or sliding sideways down the back side of the wave and getting sideways in the trough so the next wave would either roll us over or roll over us.

As the night went on, Peter and I switched tricks on the wheel every three to four hours. The other would go below, climb into the sleeping bag we shared, foul weather gear and all, and shiver himself to sleep. John stayed in the cockpit the whole time to keep Peter and me awake and he would sit huddled forward in the cockpit against the cabin bulkhead facing aft. When he saw a wave coming from an odd direction or one that was bigger than normal he would shout out to warn us. I do not remember him ever sleeping during the nights and sleeping damn little during the day and then only when Peter and I were both on deck. Both Peter and I will tell you that if it weren't for John, our least experienced sailor, we don't know how we could have kept on doing our job at the helm all that time.

It is hard to explain how it felt to be at the wheel for all those hours. It was as if we were under attack, with each wave trying new tricks to overrun us. It was never repetitious, since each wave demanded a different maneuver, an adjustment to a new sensation, a zig or a zag to narrowly escape the clutches of the sea that had turned so angry. Getting away was not always because I did the right thing every time; often it was *Tailwind* herself that rose back up to keep on fighting when I got too far up on a wave and went bow down into the wave ahead. As we went roaring down with the knot meter pegged at ten knots, the feeling was as if we had been launched like a spit ball flicked off a giant's thumb. Sometimes a wave sneaked up from behind and crashed down on us, filling the cockpit, washing forward and then back again, sloshing over the decks toward us while the overweighed stern was slow to recover to level and the knot meter was at zero. Or we would broach, sliding sideways, heeled hard to port down the back of the wave, desperately trying to keep from getting abeam of the next wave that would then try to roll us the rest of the way over. It was a personal thing for me while I was on the wheel, since the responsibility for the boat and for our survival was mine and mine alone. While on the wheel, there was no one else who could react to what was happening. The wheel couldn't always make the boat do what you were asking, but there was only that one control. So I just did the best I could, and then did it again, and again, and again, and again until each attack just blurred into the next. John, always vigilant, would ask, "Can you keep going or should I get Peter to relieve you now?" I just kept on doing my best until either I asked for relief or John just went below and got Peter no matter what I said.

I feel sure Peter would tell you he felt the same way since he fought the same fight with the same grit, determination and sense of responsibility.

We had a few interesting things happen during this wild time that added to the challenge or brought some relief.

I recall having St. Elmo's Fire (a luminescent electric glow) dance around in the rigging one night for quite a few minutes. I had never seen it before but had read about it and knew what it was. It was a very eerie experience.

I could understand why a sailor, two or three hundred years ago, would attribute it to a mystical cause.

The whole time the entire boat was leaking like a sieve from the deck so that everything in the cabin was soaked. The sleeping bags must have weighed 100 pounds. This also meant that we needed to pump the bilge every hour. Our only pump was a wall-mounted three-inch hand pump. We could get the slurping sound of an empty bilge in about two to three minutes. One time, as I went below for my time in the sack, there was some water on the floorboards. I starting pumping and seemed to be making some progress, but after ten minutes there was still water coming through the pump. I got John to come down and take over the pump so I could get a flashlight and try to find out what was happening. I started lifting the floorboards and searching though all of the damn beer, which was now mostly out of the cases with the cans afloat. When I got to the place where the mast was stepped on the keel, I found the problem. Just forward on the port side a plank end was loose from the rib. And each time the boat strained, a gap would appear and water would come flowing in. This was a very bad thing! My solution was to get one of my tee shirts to use as caulking, a screwdriver and a hammer to pack the tee shirt into the gap each time the boat worked and it opened. I am sure the boys at the Alden boat yard, where she was built would be horrified, but it worked and worked very well. This took a while, and John had to drive some of the seasick crew out of bed to pump during the hour or more it took to discover, "repair," and then get the bilge empty again. I reported the situation to the skipper in his bunk as corrected and we sailed the rest of that race, the next race to Venice, Florida and then back to Pensacola, and we didn't leak at all after the seas calmed. She was hauled and repaired properly once we got home. Another one of those magic request chits was all it took.

Once our cook roused himself to fill his duties and make the three of us something to eat. He stayed below, occasionally popping his head out of the companionway to get a breath and reset his vertigo button. And after awhile, much to our pleasant surprise, he handed up three hot steaks he had fried. We ate them like starving lions and, within about three minutes, back up they came, over the rail and accompanied by our understanding that our bodies were telling us "Hey, stupid, I can't eat stuff like that; we're not feeling well either down here."

Towards the end of the second night the wind and seas had started to come down. John came below to wake me up. "You had better get up and come topside; something is going on with Peter." I came up and Peter began to explain to me that I needed to get that goddamned witch down out of the rigging. It was not fair for her to be yelling all these insults at him all the time. He would then start yelling at her to get to hell off the boat. Fatigue, saltwater ingestion, and little food had taken its toll. John and I knew we were probably not far behind him. I took over and explained to Peter that I could get the witch to leave as soon as he went below and got to sleep. We also had one of the seasick members stumble on deck for some fresh air and quickly inform us that we should be careful not to hit the line of telephone poles just to our starboard. We learned later that we were not the only boat to have incidents of hallucinations. A member of *Niki's* crew had to be restrained from going over the side to get aboard the Greyhound Bus that had come along side on its way to Pensacola. During the rest of the night John had to take some time on the wheel to give me some relief. My instruction was to do his best to keep her within thirty degrees of course one side or the other. Again he did what he needed to do. Finally the sun came up, the rain and the cloud cover were gone, and the seas and wind were down to a safe, if not a calm, state. I had John wake the skipper and tell him he needed to be on deck. When he came up with some of the others, we put sail back on and changed course to my recommended heading for St. Petersburg, based on my estimated position, which showed us well west and further south than we wanted to be.

When I gave the skipper the wheel, he asked me to explain my course, which he deemed to be too northerly. I got out the charts, went over all my plots and their rationale, but he remained sure that there was no way we could be that far west or south. So he set course due east, figuring we would spot land near or a little south of St. Petersburg. I did not have the ability at that point to argue with him or to do anything other than collapse and sleep. For the first time in more than two days John, Peter, and I were asleep at the same time. All three of us had immersion foot. Our feet had swollen to more than double their normal size. It was at least four or five days before we could wear shoes again. Our hands were raw and every part of our bodies ached. We were dehydrated. We didn't have bottled water in those days, and beer and soda had no appeal. All the spray we constantly were getting hit with surely had caused us to ingest a lot of saltwater, and we had only had some oranges to eat, not counting the ill-fated steak.

Later that morning when I awoke it was like the nightmare was over; maybe it was a dream and not real. But one look in Peter's or John's eyes and there was no doubt we knew we had just taken a turn in hell and come out the other side.

When I went topside it was a warm and pleasant day to be sailing. All hands seemed quite relaxed and happy. I saw one of them with one of the new seven transistor portable radios, trying to tune into a station to listen to some music. I immediately realized that we had had the newest electronic navigation gear on board and had never even known it. I immediately told him to stop worrying about music and to keep listening to the station until he could identify where it was located. After about fifteen minutes he knew he had a St. Petersburg station tuned in. It was weak but it was all I needed to rotate the radio and find the null point, or orientation of the radio, where the signal was the weakest. Using the compass, but keeping the radio away from it, I was able to get an accurate heading to St. Petersburg. The course was almost northwest, and, with this new information, there was no arguing that it was not correct. We didn't know yet how far away we were because it wasn't until the next morning that we were able to get two other stations and get a good triangulated fix. When I did get the fix, it was apparent that my dead reckoning showed that the skipper was correct about my position being wrong, but it was off because we were even further south and west than my estimated fix. The wind and the current had exceeded the estimate of every boat in the race, but *Niki*, with her new direction finder, was the first to realize it, and she made the correction as soon as the weather would allow and won the race by going the shortest distance. It was not until 2010, when the BP oil platform exploded and oil began to gush into the Gulf of Mexico that I and most of the rest of the world learned about the loop current. It most surely also played a part in our getting so far to the south.

Just after we corrected our course and had all the sails trimmed, a small brown sparrow landed on the deckhouse. We were amazed. How did he get way out here so far from shore? We realized that he was a fellow survivor of the storm. He must have been out fighting the same fight we had and could have barely believed his eyes when suddenly he saw us out there in the middle of nowhere. He probably figured it was all over, but he too came out the other side of hell. He stayed with us almost all the way to the yacht club docks. He ate from our hands and perched on us. After what he had been through, he was without fear.

We finally came across the finish line at about midnight Monday in fifth, or last place, a fact reported this way in the newspaper but adamantly disputed by John Longdin to this day. It seemed like a week, and it was with a great sigh of relief the next morning, after spending time aground in the bay, that we threw a line to a tender to tow us into the dock and to the relaxed safety of the St. Petersburg yacht club. A twenty-eight foot sloop was the last one in and claimed to have seen Cuba; they were blown so far south. I would not have wanted to be in their place; it was tough enough aboard the forty-four foot *Tailwind.*

We were a rag-tag bunch that invaded the swanky St. Petersburg Yacht Club. And the twenty young crewmembers from the two identical Navy yawls headed up the list. The first thing we did was to take every single thing off the boats to dry out. Clothes, sleeping bags, mattresses, sails, you name it, were spread all over the docks and the club's grounds. It went from yacht club to shantytown in one hour flat. Two of the crew were sent off the grounds to search out a place where we could eat and fill our starving bellies. They returned just as we finished converting the club to a style more like our own to announce they had found an All-You-Can-Eat-Buffet for something like two bucks a head. The owner of this place was in for it; he might be broke before the afternoon was done. We told him the story of where we had been and how long it had been since we had eaten. He took it in stride and took our money and we lit into it. We all got seated with mounds of food and double glasses of milk and were about to begin when one after another looked up at each other with this feeling of horror as, almost simultaneously, after sitting down and not moving we were attacked with motion sickness symptoms, called "sea legs". There we were starving, with food on our plates, and the room started to roll and pitch. We started to laugh at ourselves and within a couple of minutes were eating like the starving warriors we were.

Upon returning to the boats with our stomachs full and feeling the greatness of life, I thought that a beer might be just the thing. I took one that we had stacked on the dock and immediately noticed that it seemed light, and I don't mean "lite;" we didn't have such a thing back then. The can must have leaked. I pulled open the newfangled pop-top and, sure enough, almost a third of it was gone. Not only that. When I tasted it, there was definitely salty water in with the beer. This was a Major problem. We had finally arrived where the partying was to start and our beer was bad, to say nothing of our lost investment. This seemed to be a problem that related to the solder around the new pop-tops having been corroded by saltwater.

Just at this point I noticed an eighty-plus foot motor yacht come into the dock, tie up and discharge a group of very fancy guests, obviously arriving for luncheon at the yacht club. And, lo and behold, what do you think the name of that yacht was? *Miss Budweiser*. St Elmo, the patron saint of sailors, had delivered our salvation. I took a few of the cans and went over and requested that one of the crew ask the captain if I could speak with him. He came right down. I explained who we were and that we had just come in from the race and then showed him the problem with the beer. He understood immediately and asked how much of it we had. He was a little amazed at the figure of forty cases until he looked over and saw it piled up all over the place, and said, "I will take care of this." In about two hours here came two guys with hand trucks loaded with cases of beer onto the dock. They didn't say a word, stacked the cases, and took away all they could of the bad beer until we had forty new cases of Budweiser and no more cans of Busch. I looked over at *Miss Budweiser*, which was just pulling away from the dock, and caught the skipper's eye. He saluted and then turned his attention back to boat handling.

The wild time was over but we had another race to Venice, Florida and then our trip back to Pensacola before we were to return to our lives of continuing to become naval aviators.

In about two days we had our gear pretty well dried out and re-stowed aboard. I am sure the yacht club was glad to have our mess gone and to be looking its normal shipshape self again. There were receptions and dinners for the end of the first race and more for the start of the next. Peter, John and I had to go barefoot as our feet were still swollen, but it didn't matter. Everyone was wonderful and treated this bunch of young Navy officers and cadets like royalty. I don't think any of us could pay for a drink and were continually being introduced to the eligible women who seemed to litter the place.

The race to Venice, about sixty miles to the south, was to take place on Friday night with a start at about sunset and an expected arrival Saturday morning for more festivities at their club. This yacht club life could grow on you. There were a lot more boats in this race, since a number of boats from the Venice club had sailed up and the St. Pete boats could sail back home on Sunday, making it a weekend event. All went smoothly as we got the start off in light winds and slowly made our way out of Tampa Bay into the gulf. The light winds kept all of us pretty well bunched up and we could see navigation lights all around us. After about an hour the wind completely stopped and we were all bobbing around becalmed. It was not long after that, as the air cooled, that we had a pea soup fog engulf us all, a complete reversal from a few days ago when we were scrambling to just hold on.

This was old and boring for everyone. You could hear every sound from every boat and every word that was spoken. I had to think up something to make a little excitement. Since no one could see anyone else, the only way you knew what anyone was doing was by the boat noise and what people were saying to each other. During this period, pretty well everyone realized that anything they said was being heard by all, and that realization gradually caused most to shut up and be quiet. I am sure there were also a number sleeping as well, which was certainly the case aboard the *Tailwind*.

This was what I did. In complete silence I went from one crewmember to the next with my finger to my lips and whispered my plan to them. Each was given a duty and where in the action they fit. It took about fifteen minutes to get everyone ready and answer all the questions and make the suggested changes that would increase the effect.

With a nod we began. The first man grabbed the boom and made the slightest of moves making the sail flop ever so little. None of us moved. After a minute, a little bigger shake of the boom and the sail was a little louder. None of us moved. A voice from another boat asked, "Did you hear that? Listen." None of us moved. After waiting a minute, another even more pronounced shake of the boom. Back came the voice, "Hear that? A breeze just moved a sail." We knew that these comments were heard by everyone and every ear would be tuned up to the max and all were getting ready for a break in this boredom. It was time to make our move so I gave another nod to the boom-shaker to start making the "wind" increase.

I started yelling at the crew to get to their stations. Commotion erupted as they ran around. The sheets went on the winches and they made their whirring sounds as the sheets were hauled in. Then, with a wave of my hand, all motion stopped and we went dead silent.

It worked. There was pandemonium throughout the fleet with yelling and hollering going on everywhere and crews moving about. At this point we were all busting a gut and dying, trying not to laugh out loud. It wasn't too long until all you could hear was "What the hell happened?" "What is going on?" "Who got that breeze and where did they go?" A little after that we could hear people beginning to realize they had been had. Some actually got mad as hell, but most started to laugh, our signal that we could finally escape blowing ourselves up and laugh out loud too. We never admitted anything, but, when we got to Venice, the word leaked out. I think somebody was too proud of having pulled this off to not take the credit. But it wasn't me.

Of course, finally a real breeze came up and the fog lifted and we proceeded to Venice. It was a relaxing sail and had us all ready for the parties that were to follow. On Sunday many of us were invited to members' homes for picnics and barbecues, I got to go water skiing, which I had not done in a couple of years, and I enjoyed showing off.

The two Navy yawls left late that afternoon to head home. The weather was ideal with fifteen knots of breeze from the east and seas of two to three feet. We settled in as darkness began to fall. Peter, John and I pretty much considered ourselves passengers for this ride and went below to sleep for hours and hours.

When we got up in the morning there was the wonderful smell of bacon in the cabin and our faithful cook was outdoing himself. After a leisurely breakfast I went topside. *Alert* was nowhere in sight, having gotten over the horizon in one direction or another during the night. I lay on the deck propped on a pillow and read while I soaked up the warm sun. At noon, sandwiches and a beer were delivered. This was good, very, very, good.

That afternoon a pod of thirty or forty porpoises (they were not called dolphins in those days) came into our bow wake. They stayed for hours as we lay on our stomachs with our heads over the rail watching them roll, play, jump, and generally have a ball. It was the first time I ever saw them come right up to the boat and play. I was mesmerized and couldn't take my eyes off them.

The afternoon and evening continued in this pleasant fashion with a great dinner, beer, lots of stories and lies told with the accompanying riotous laughter of good friends.

I awoke the next morning to find us in a near calm sea with only occasional small breaths of wind. We could see a mast near the horizon and assumed it must be *Alert*. We weren't getting anywhere fast so we took advantage of every movement of air to move toward *Alert*. After awhile they were doing the same toward us. Remember that there were no VHF radios with which to chat them up and make a plan. About mid-afternoon we came along side each other. After a little chatter we realized neither of was going anywhere so we started comparing dinner plans and were soon rafted up out there in the middle of the Gulf of Mexico in a flat sea. We began swimming and, of course, drinking beer that was the temperature of the bilge, where we could safely store our non pop-top cans. After an hour or so we looked up to find an old and seriously beat up commercial fishing boat approaching.

They came up alongside and asked, "Is everything okay?" We assured them it was and they responded, "We weren't sure and began to think that maybe there was something wrong with you. It's pretty strange seeing identical boats tied up together floating around out here in the middle of the Gulf." We hadn't thought of it from their perspective, but we were pretty strange-looking, although it might not be so strange in the high-flying, pot-smuggling days that would follow in a few years.

An idea struck me. They would have ice on board; so I asked if they would like to trade some ice for a case of beer. It was quickly realized that they thought that would be a damn good idea. We threw them a line and then put a case of beer in a pillowcase and tied it to the line and they pulled it over to themselves while we fed out line so the bag would stay high and dry. In a few minutes back came the pillowcase, straining at the seams full of big chunks of ice. They hollered to tell us to send the bag back over, which we did. They soon sent it back and it had two big groupers in it that were still wiggling. They had to be twenty to thirty pounds each. We were delighted and let them know it by putting another case of beer in the bag and sending it back to them.

I asked why they were way out here to fish and they answered, "We fish a high hump on the bottom that holds these grouper." "Well, how do you find that hump out here in the middle of nowhere?" I asked. "We just put our anchor down when we get near and, when it takes a bite, we start to fish," he answered, as they turned to head back. Sure enough, there was the anchor line, hanging over the bow. GPS be damned.

Our cook came through with those two fish. We rigged the spinnaker pole and hung the barbecue from it and swung it over the side. I don't know what he did make that fish so delicious, but I will never have a better dinner in a better location with better company than I had that night.

We slowly drifted apart as a breeze started to come up. The next afternoon we sailed into the wet slip at Pensacola, different men then had left a couple of weeks before.

I can see now how this chance discovery of *Tailwind* on a Sunday afternoon and the adventures that it led me to would provide me with experiences that allowed me to succeed in overcoming the incredible challenges I encountered during my service in Viet Nam and during the rest of my life.

At Sea

When you are at sea, alone in your thoughts, sharing with all that is the world, what moves and exists on its own, unconquered by the efforts and forces of man, you become disconnected from the world where you normally live, a world where man is lulled into thinking he has control over his destiny. You can no longer pretend you have any power. You can only dance to the music being played. The sea can do as she pleases and you can only do your best as you fight and struggle to stay alive, for she surely has no regard for you. Propelled by only the forces of nature, there is no choice but to believe. To have ridden aboard the forces of nature, to the edge of where life and death touch, is to live life to the fullest and to be comfortable in giving up your sense of control to the forces and the power that surround you.

Vol. 2, No 1   PENSACOLA, FLORIDA   February 1965

Official U.S. Navy Color Photo by Rosenthal-Yawls "NIKKI" and "TAILWIND" vie for position.

Nikki & Tailwind

Tailwind

More information and photos at
www.klondikeplayboy.com

The Newest Second Lieutenant

The job of learning to fly and becoming a commissioned officer was done. I was now a second lieutenant and the 7,968ᵗʰ naval aviator as I began a new life as an officer and gentleman. The term officer and gentleman is something I have never taken lightly and have accepted as a responsibility every since. If I say I will do it, it will be done. If I say it is so, it is the truth, the whole truth and nothing but the truth. To classify someone as an officer and a gentleman is to describe a person with the highest possible ethical standards. It does not assure they will always be right, but it does assure they will never try to do wrong. Nor does it mean that that you will always follow the rules.

Not only was I going to my new duty station, MCAS New River in North Carolina, but I was also on my way back to Connecticut to be married to the girl I had made my fiancée before leaving for the Marine Corps. We had only seen each other three times since I had left two years earlier.

I was going to be driving the well-worn 1955 Chevy that I had bought to replace my motor scooter when I left Saufley Field to move on to Whiting Field. I had the car packed with what little gear I had, but I did not get all the final paperwork done and my orders in hand until late in the afternoon. No matter, I had to get started on my way to Jacksonville, NC since I could not be late. I had already postponed my marriage date twice, due somewhat to weather but, I must admit, mostly due to sailing. It was now set for the following Saturday, July 24th. In fact I was supposed to have been married the Saturday before, and all the napkins, match books, etc., had July 10, 1965 printed on them, and it was now Monday the 19th.

It was about two in the morning on a dark and stormy night. There was no direct Interstate on this route in 1965. However, at the point in the trip that I was in Fayetteville, North Carolina on a four-lane road with a wide grass median, I must have fallen asleep, since suddenly I was in the median, spinning, with mud and grass flying everywhere. There was, of course, no air conditioning so the vent window was open to allow some air in during the rain. Enough mud got though that small opening to coat everything inside the car. And, of course, the motor died and would not start. I got out and, lo and behold, I was right in front of the main gate to Pope Air Force Base. I walked up to the guardhouse; one side of me completely coated in mud, pointed to my car, and explained my circumstances. The guard was from the motor pool and said he would have one of his buddies get a wrecker to tow me up to the parking lot just inside the gate. It wasn't twenty minutes later and they had me under the lights in the parking lot. I lifted the hood and it was easy to see why the car wouldn't start. The whole engine compartment was packed with mud and grass. The tow truck driver helped me clean it out, and I was able to get the motor started. The car and I were in rough shape at this point, but I had to keep going.

After an hour it was apparent that the generator was not putting out enough juice since the headlights were fading to a dim glow as I reached the last of the battery's power. I needed to stop, but it would have to be on a hill so I could roll down to restart the car without a battery when the sun came up and I wouldn't need the headlights to see. A hill is no easy thing to find in the eastern Carolinas, but I finally found a hump in a parking lot leading to a warehouse, backed in, fell immediately asleep for about three hours, and awoke in daylight. I rolled down the hump, popped the clutch, and was back on my way again.

I arrived at New River and located my friend John Longdin, while I left the car running. He told me how to get to his place so I could shower, sleep and be able to shut off the car since he could give me a jump start. The next day was Wednesday and I had to get checked in. I learned that my squadron assignment was to be VMO-1 and, of course, filled out lots of paperwork.

I again spent the night at John's, got a jump-start in the morning, and drove to the Jacksonville airport. The car was going to stay there for a while, and it was no longer on my list of things to worry about. It had gotten me to where I needed to be to start the last leg of the trip home to Connecticut and my wedding.

I arrived in Connecticut on Thursday afternoon to learn that I had to meet the Catholic priest because I needed special dispensation to marry my Catholic fiancée since I had not received the prerequisite instruction. I got through that somehow; the priest must have been deaf and blind to let a heathen like me marry one of his flock.

A rehearsal dinner, a wedding, a driving honeymoon to Niagara Falls and Chicago, and back home in what seemed like a flash. We packed Beverly's stuff into the 1961 Chevy that had been my Grandmother's and was now her wedding present to us, and we headed to our new life as a married couple in the Marine Corps. We did make one more stop at the New York World's Fair before heading to Jacksonville.

It was no time at all before we found a furnished place in which to live, Beverly got a job teaching in a grammar school, and I was hard at work learning to fly UH-1Es at VMO-1. By the way, Beverly got paid $3,200 dollars a year, and that's what we lived on. Every dollar I made went into savings. We had a lot of fun and had everything we wanted or needed. Not only did we do this during this first stint at VMO-1, but we also did the same when I returned from Viet Nam back to VMO-1. Of course, we did have more money that year since Beverly's pay was now $3,400.

Survival Training

It was not long after the first planes began to fly that it was learned that there are times when they may have to land in places you have not anticipated. A motor stopped, a part fell off, or somebody shot you down and, either you landed then and there, or, even worse, you jumped or were ejected and you landed via parachute someplace other than where the plane landed. In that these unanticipated places were not usually the parking lot of a Holiday Inn, a pilot might be required to fend for himself well away from civilization and maybe in an area that the enemy controlled. "Pilots fending for themselves" is nearly an oxymoron. We live the good life. Fending-for-yourself type of living is what grunts do. This meant that to learn these skills pilots would have to be dragged away from their officer's clubs and their air-conditioned ready rooms to be taught how to live in the woods on their own.

I had been a boy scout and was raised in the country, so facing this experience as part of my flight training was not too horrifying for me. But there were a fair number of city boys that had only seen a tree in the local park and maybe had actually been on a picnic only once or twice as their total experience with nature. Like it or not, all of the flight students had to face the trip to Eglin Air Force base, about forty miles east of Pensacola, where there was a survival school on part of their thousands of acres of piney woods.

I learned one lesson in the four days and three nights we spent "surviving," and that is if you think there are some things you would never eat, you have never been REALLY hungry. By the third evening we were camping near a pond. I am sure we had had something to eat but I do not remember it and we were all feeling not only hunger but also the weakness and exhaustion that hunger causes. We were hiking every day and expending lots of energy. While I was digging next to the stream on the last night, trying to find something to use as bait to catch a fish, I found water chestnuts growing wild in the mud. You would have thought I had come across a McDonalds, I was so excited. I collected them and, as I was taking them back to the camp site, I spotted a snake. It didn't take more than a second for me to step on it, pull my knife and cut off its head. Things were really looking up. The four of us on our team were going to have meat and vegetable soup that night. As we were preparing our meal, I spotted a mouse running for cover and again leapt into action and stomped on him—more meat for the stew. I know you are curling your lip in disgust as you read this and saying there is no way you would ever eat snake and mouse stew. You are saying that for just one reason—you have never been REALLY hungry. It was not an epicurean delight, to be sure, but we ate every last drop.

The next survival exercise I went on was in North Carolina while in VMO-1. This was shorter and there are no disgusting dietary aspects to this tale. This exercise was only two days and one night and took place near the Cherry Point MCAS about thirty miles north of New River. Again there were four men to a team and about four teams that were scattered far enough apart so that we didn't know where the other teams were. We set up camp with our piece of parachute and settled in for the night. It kept getting colder and colder and soon we four were all huddled together in one ball doing our best to stay warm. The only complaining heard about this unmanly behavior was "I've been on the outside edge of this love fest long enough and it's time to let me into the middle." We also had a one-man rubber raft that we were all trying to use as a blanket. It wouldn't cover one person so it was of pretty limited value and was often slowly slid from one to another until that person got caught.

Our mission for the next day was to use our map and compass to navigate from our camp to a barrier beach on the Atlantic where we would be picked up by the Cherry Point SAR H-34. The territory we had to cross was being held by "the enemy," who would be patrolling in search of downed aviators, and we had to make our escape while evading these patrols or we would be "arrested" and thrown into "prison camp."

The sun was slowly bringing up the temperature from the high thirties towards what would be comfortable in the low sixties by afternoon. We gathered our equipment, which consisted primarily of the parachute material, parachute cord and the rubber raft, which was going to be a critical item since we were going to have to cross a river about a hundred yards wide. Swimming across was not a desirable option due to the temperature. We cautiously began to move out. We took turns having one of us move as silently as possible, keeping his eyes peeled for any sign of the "enemy" while the other three carried the gear and waited for the all clear sign before they caught up. After we had traveled two or three miles through the woods, we came upon a dirt road with about a hundred yards of tall grass, almost four feet high, between the tree line and the road. It was my turn as point so I got down on my belly and used my elbows to crawl slowly and silently to the edge of the road. When I arrived, I slowly parted the grass at the edge of the road, brought my face up to look each way and what I saw froze me into complete stillness. Not six inches to the left of my face was a guard, squatting down on his haunches, smoking a cigarette. Miraculously he did not see me or hear me, but there was no way I could move even an inch without being caught, so all I could do was hold up and wave my other hand to warn the others to get back into the woods and hide.

This suspense went on for at least five minutes until the guard finally stood up, threw down his cigarette butt, looked down to grind it out with his foot, saw me and leapt straight up into the air and partially out of his skin. Seeing me just six inches away was such a shock it took a moment for him to get fully back into his skin and react. I was "arrested" immediately. He wanted to know where the rest of my team was but, of course, I lied through my teeth and told him I had been lost for over an hour and had no idea where they were.

He took me off to the "prison camp," which was not too bad. There were four others in prison with me—one whole team. They gave me a cup of coffee and told me I would have to stay there about forty-five minutes and then would be released with the others to continue our trek to the beach for pickup. The one hitch was that they were going to take all the gear away from all of us, including the team's rubber raft. This was not a good thing.

The time was up and we were let go. I had only one goal in mind and that was to find my team members before they all got across that river. I wanted to ride across the river in the raft. I took off at a trot, headed toward the river and where I thought they would be trying to cross. My fellow prisoners seemed to have no plan at all so were more or less staying in my wake. I soon came to the edge of a wooded cliff that looked down onto the river.

I could see about a mile of the river from this vantage point as it snaked its way between hills about seventy-five to a hundred feet high on each side with about a hundred yards of tall marsh reeds between the base of the hills and the river. To my everlasting joy I could see three guys just starting out into the reeds from the base of the hill. It had to be my boys and they had a raft. I couldn't yell to them or I would be back in "prison," so I took off, running around the hilltop to the point where they had been starting into the reeds, ran down the hill, then into the path they had made by beating the reeds into submission, and then slogged through the mud after them. Their having made a path made my trip over this hundred yards a lot easier and faster. I caught up to them just as they arrived at the river's edge and were starting to make plans about how to get to the other side. They were happy to see me, but that did not last too long when my other four prison mates came slogging into view. Now there were eight of us and one raft. My team quickly set the others straight. We would be going over first and then they could have the raft and would be on their own.

The plan we settled on was to tie a piece of parachute cord to the front and to the back of the one-man raft. Then the first man would paddle with his hands to the other side while we kept hold of the end of the cord on our side. He would get out when he landed and hold the end of his cord on his side, and we would pull the raft back to our side. This way there would be no more paddling and each crossing would go a lot quicker, being propelled by the cords rather than being hand paddled. All agreed and number one got aboard and started paddling across. It was not pretty, but he finally made it and scrambled out onto the other shore.

Just as we were about to start to pull the raft back to our side we heard an outboard motor coming down the river at a high rate of speed. The guards were patrolling the river and we were about to be captured again. We pulled the raft back to us as fast as we could and, of course, our man on the other side had to let go of his rope so the patrol boat didn't snag it. We got everyone on our side backed away from the edge so we wouldn't be seen, and soon the boat with two guards came into view. Just as they were in front of us, our man on the other side started hooting and hollering and thrashing through the reeds. We couldn't believe our ears or our eyes. Did this guy go insane or what? Thankfully the guards could not hear the commotion, due to the loud outboard motor noise, and missed seeing the reeds being stomped to death. They just kept on going downriver. We had gotten away with it. We then had to do one more paddle across by hand but the system worked like a charm after that.

As soon as the fifth man got to the other side, we first four, as agreed, left them and started to the beach. This was, of course, after we had tried to torture the first man for his stupidity and for having nearly gotten us all captured. Well, it turns out he had a pretty good excuse. As he had moved back from the river's edge, he had almost stepped on an alligator. He was not a Carolina swamp native so didn't realize that, with the temperature this low, gators are very, very slow. It was also only about three feet long and was surely as afraid of our man as our man was afraid of him. The gator was still there, where he had moved back away from the action, so we knew he hadn't made up the story, and we had to agree that, under the circumstances, we would have probably done the same thing.

The four of us set off for the final leg of our escape. We were not drenched but we were all damp around the edges, especially our feet, lower legs and arms. We climbed up the hill to the north before we turned again to go east to the Atlantic. We were shocked to step out of the woods at the top of the hill onto a golf course. It was empty since the sun was beginning its descent and the chill was rapidly coming back. It was less than an hour after we were on the golf course when we came out of the woods again to see the ocean and a ragtag group milling around about a quarter of a mile further down the beach. We soon joined them, and before very long the stories started to roll about who had had it the worst. The alligator story won hands down. Soon all the groups were together with the instructors and we all were waiting for the SAR bird to come and get us. We were getting colder and colder as time passed. Finally the instructors got word on their radio that a jet out of Cherry Point had gone into the drink and the SAR bird was on a real mission, and we would have to wait.

We got a fire going and did the best we could to keep warm. This went on for about three hours and there were no happy campers any more, although for sure none of us were even close to thinking the SAR bird should be doing anything other than finding the downed pilot. If it had been one of us, we knew which priority we would be opting for.

We learned via the radio that, thankfully, the SAR bird was able to find the ejected pilot, pick him up and return him to base and that they were now on the way to pick us up. This immediately raised our morale as we knew there was going to be an end to this misery soon and especially since the pilot had been recovered.

Soon the bird arrived and took the first of two trips to get us back. You would guess right if you figured I got the second lift as my ride. I was as near to being frozen as I'd ever been. Driving home seemed to take hours, and, when I did finally arrive, I got in a hot shower and didn't get out until all the hot water was gone.

Camping in any form has had no appeal to me since, and I am sure you now know why.

Grab Ass Training

I had been in the Marine Corps for over two years before I received my first official introduction and training in the art of grab ass, specifically aviation grab ass. In case you are not familiar with the term "grab ass," it is basically dicking around, screwing off, or any activity counter to being productive, and always something that will meet with the disapproval of anyone in authority. In other words, having fun.

Having a helicopter at your disposal for grab ass activities, as you may imagine, provides tremendous opportunities not available to lesser grab ass artists. In fact, it was not until I received my first lesson in aviation grab ass that I even considered the fantastic potential for fun and games that could be devised when you could use a helicopter.

My introduction came about completely unexpectedly when I was stationed with VMO-1 to learn to fly UH-1Es. I do not want to infer that I was not fully familiar with all kinds of terrestrial grab ass-type activities. In fact, I had been an active practitioner of the art since early in my childhood. However, I had never heard it called by its proper name until boot camp at Parris Island, where even letting your eye balls roam off center was classified as grab ass by my drill instructor. In fact, I had a Major hiatus in any fun-related grab ass until boot camp was well over. Let's get back to my introduction to aviation grab ass or the stories will never end.

UH-1Es were new to VMO-1 and were still being delivered when I arrived. Even the saltiest pilots who were our instructors were getting familiar with the nuances and details of the new bird. When it came to strapping machine guns and rocket pods on to a helicopter, it was all new for everybody.

Late one afternoon after I had been in the squadron a number of months, I was the co-pilot on a gunnery training flight late one afternoon with one of the saltier pilots, Captain Lowery. He was a very senior captain with very little stick up his butt. He had been my instructor for numerous training flights previously and was a great help in making me proficient, while instilling in me what a great bird the UH-1E was when you knew how to treat her. He also was a full participant in most Friday night happy hours and kept us new kids in the loop so we felt like part of the VMO-1 family.

The gunnery range was, and still is, on Brown's Island, in the Intracoastal Waterway just north of the New River Inlet. There was an old wreck of a truck and a dumpster for us to aim at. The island was covered with brush except for occasional bare patches of sand here and there. It was here we learned tricks like keeping your rudders set so the ball was on dead center, showing you had no yaw. If not, the machine gun rounds and rockets would be going anywhere but where you had pointed them. In fact, when it came to the rockets, we all learned that, no matter what you did, they were going pretty much anywhere they felt

89

like going. During these practice flights the crew chiefs and gunners were also getting their training. As we pulled out after each run, they would use their door guns to shoot at the targets. As you can imagine, these were favorite hops for us all. Flying and shooting at the same time—it was hard to get better than that. It would not be more than a couple of months after this that I would learn that it was not anywhere near as much fun when somebody on the ground was shooting back at you.

All was going well and we had made about three or four runs when, as we were pulling out, a deer broke out of the brush and was running in the open. Lowery went nuts. "I got, I got," he yelled, and we wheeled over on our nose and dove at the deer with the guns blazing. The deer disappeared into another clump of brush and appeared not to have been hit. Well, I didn't know it at the time, but I was now getting my very first lesson in aviation grab ass and, it turned out, from a master of the art with long standing.

The hunt was on. You would think a deer against a helicopter with four side-mounted and two door-mounted swivel 7.62 machine guns would not stand a chance and this would be over in a flash. Well, you'd be wrong. Lowery, relying on his years of hunting experience, knew right away that, if you can't see the deer, you can't shoot it. So his next move was to get right down on the top of the bushes and hover around until he finally scared the crap out of the deer and it would break out into the open. I will have to admit that the other three of us onboard knew we were in the presence of a true grab ass artist and were pretty much in shock and awe at this point.

Well, the hovering plan worked; out burst the deer, running like a bat out of hell, from under the right side of the bird, which was Lowery's and the gunner's side. Lowery started yelling at the gunner to shoot, shoot, shoot. The rounds started ripping out and the deer bobbed and wove like a well-trained Marine and disappeared into another growth of brush, again unharmed. This same routine happened two more times, with the deer always breaking out to our right. After the second time the gunner didn't hit it, Lowery had the crew chief take over that gun. Same deal: deer breaks right, bobs and weaves for fifty to seventy-five yards, and gets away untouched. We had probably shot 200-300 rounds at this point and Lowery was about to have a cow.

"God damn it, Boden; get your goddamned ass out of that goddamned seat, get back there on that goddamned gun, and show these goddamned blind bastards how to do it," Lowery yells. Of course, "God damn it" was not the actual word he used. I pulled my microphone cord and climbed over the center console to take over the gun from the crew chief. We looked at each other and rolled our eyes. What else were we supposed to do but what we were told? I hadn't shot a machine gun since a one-hour training and familiarization session at Camp Geiger during infantry training, but who cared; at this point it was all about ego. So, in we go for the fifth time to chase the deer out of the cover, and, as usual, after a couple of minutes of bouncing around on the top of the bushes, out it came right under me. I let go a burst as it headed down the beach about fifty feet from the water. Whack. Down it went with half its hind-quarter blown away, dead as a door nail. It went down right in front of

91

a stake with a NO TRESPASSING sign on it. Would you believe it? Lowery was ecstatic. He lands next to the deer and tells me to get back in the co-pilot seat. I jumped out, ran around the front and climbed back into the seat the normal way, through the door. As soon as I had plugged my helmet back into the intercom I heard, "Boden, you got the bird. Just hold it right here while I get out and field dress this thing. Crew chief, come with me." "I got it," I replied, and out he goes with the crew chief right behind him. He pulls his knife, makes a cut to open the tendon just above the hoof on one rear leg, and slips the other rear hoof between the tendon and the bone. Then he motioned the crew chief to help lift the deer, and they hung it by the rear legs on the NO TRESPASSING sign. In less than one minute he had slit the throat and the belly and had the guts out. Field stripped, zip zap. He and the crew chief climbed back in, and Lowery started waving his arm for me to take off even before he had strapped in or plugged back into the intercom.

On the flight back, after lots of kudos for my fine shooting, he laid out the plan. We were going back to the squadron; the crew was to jump out quickly and go get us a couple of jugs of water and rags. We would leave the crew there since he didn't want to get their asses any deeper into this, just in case the whole deal went south. You can also bet he swore them, and me, to absolute silence with the threat of indescribable horrors if he ever heard about this from anybody else. With rags and water aboard we got clearance from the tower and took off again for Brown's Island. We landed, he jumped out, threw the deer into the back, and off we went. He, of course, had a plan. He landed in a clearing that was just off a dirt road and not far from the base. He got out, got the deer out, used the water and rags to get rid of any evidence, and then back we went to the base. He immediately went to his car and left while I filled out the yellow sheet. That was the last I heard about it, and I sure didn't retell the story for many years. I never got any venison either; but with a wink Lowery often bought me a beer at happy hour.

Real World to Viet Nam

In May, after ten months at North Carolina in VMO-1, I was officially trained "In-Type," had my orders, and reality was at hand. It was time to go to war. Lots of arrangements were made. My wife was going back to Connecticut and returning to college. The movers were arriving and taking our things, and the parties to say goodbye were over. I was to report to Treasure Island in San Francisco, for transport to Viet Nam. To save money, Ron Corley, John Arick and I were going to meet in Washington, DC and then drive a car across the country for a company that made that type of arrangements. So my wife and I stopped in DC, where she dropped me off before continuing north to Connecticut. The three couples said their goodbyes; we got into the car waving goodbye and drove off.

The trip was of little excitement. One issue we had not counted on was a lack of space. The girl that owned the car had filled the trunk completely with her stuff, which meant that our three fully-packed sea bags as well as the three of us had to fit in the passenger compartment. This left a small hole in the back seat which we took turns fitting into. There was much complaining from the back seat, no matter whose turn it was. One night we stopped at our usual flea bag-quality motel since we were determined to do the trip on the cheap as we had a couple of activities planned where our money would be spent on things that were "required" of all officers on their way to Viet Nam. More on that later. We had the motel deliver a roll-away bed to allow the one room to accommodate the three of us. It was my turn in the roll-away that night. We got ready, and I unfolded my bed, got situated, and climbed in. It immediately folded back up, making it look like I had just been consumed by an alligator. After about a two-second pause, the three of us started laughing so hard we could barely breathe. For the rest of the trip and even years afterwards, John would break out laughing because the picture of me being eaten by the alligator had just floated through his mind.

On the last stop in Reno before reaching Treasure Island I had my first opportunity to gamble. I had read and studied a system to play craps and was ready to learn the joy of winning money. This turned out very well. My system was to bet the field and double my next bet after each time I lost. This was really working, and I was up $128 on my original one dollar bet. I watched a number of people at the game who got very excited every time they won. I didn't get it; this was not that much fun. Having more money than I came in with was nice, but not so great as to be jumping up and down and squealing. I kept at it and soon the tide of good fortune turned away from me. I lost a bet, so I bet two, then four, then eight, then thirty two and then the rest of my money—sixty four dollars. I don't need to tell you what happened, and you can be damned sure I didn't bet $128 of my own hard-earned money to keep the system going. Guess what. If I had, it, too, would have been gone. When I started this story I told you it worked out very well. Was I nuts? I didn't win anything. But it did work out well, because at the tender age of twenty-two I learned that winning money gambling didn't give me the big rush that it seemed to give some people and that when I lost money I felt like crying. It didn't take much of my brain power to realize I would never be a gambler so that was the end for me. I am sure that decision has saved me one huge pile of money during the ensuing forty-five years.

The next day we arrived in Treasure Island and began the endless paperwork that seemed to appear in floods as soon as you got near any guy who had a rack of rubber stamps on his desk. This would take a couple of days and we had our evenings free. One of the "required" activities I spoke of earlier was to see "The Twin Peaks of San Francisco." The place to do this was at the Condor Club, where Carol Doda was a topless stripper, famous in the 1960s and through the 1980s. Carol was one of the first of that era to make international news by having her bust enhanced, which went from a size 34 to 44 with silicone injections. Her breasts were sometimes also referred to as Doda's "twin 44s." Mission accomplished, and a true sight to behold.

Soon we were off on the twelve-plus hour flight to Okinawa, to be met by another round of paperwork and rubber stamps and boring lectures. We were housed in temporary barracks whose only unusual feature was that, when we left it the morning after a rain that first night, there were hundreds and hundreds of snails all over the outside walls. These were no garden-variety snails; they would have been called *escargots* if they were in France—extra-large *escargots* at that.

While we were there we were able to fulfill our second "required" activity, which was to have a steam bath and massage with a masseuse who walked on your back, using her toes and heels on your muscles. We were having a great time with a couple of beers before we began. This was the first time I had ever had a steam bath or a massage and was really enjoying it. As we finished and were getting dressed, Ron realized his watch was missing. This took all the joy out of this new experience for him and he was madder than hell. Here he was, one day in the Orient and the bastards had got at him already. I don't know how long it took him to get over it, but it was not during the next few days before we went on to our separate squadrons. So I had formed two impressions of the Far-East in my first two days there: that steam baths and massages are great but be careful of your valuables, and that there were a lot of huge snails everywhere. Thank goodness I was able to see a lot more of it and learn that Asians are incredible people, and that being different doesn't make us better.

Within two days we began the next leg of our journey. We boarded a C-130 that was set up with four rows of cloth strip bench seats that ran fore and aft. This meant that you sat with your knees sort of interlocked with the knees of the guy you were looking at across the nonexistent aisle. We were pretty much packed in like sardines and would be this way for about five hours while we flew the 1,400 miles to Da Nang. Off we went and within less than an hour were into storms and very rough air. The word came back that the pressurization was out and we were not going to be able to climb out of it. And, oh, we're sorry, we don't expect to break out

97

of the weather until a couple of hundred miles from Da Nang.

It was not long before the vomiting began, and there was no place for it to go but between our legs and onto the floor as we wiggled our feet and knees to avoid getting it on our own lap from the guy sitting opposite us. As you can imagine, many who were just managing to keep from getting sick lost it when somebody else's vomit got on him. Often it would look as if we were watching a case of the dueling vomiters. I managed to keep not only from vomiting but also from being vomited on. There were a few aviators who lost the fight, however. A large majority of us were smokers and even vomit was not going to overcome the desire for a cigarette. After lighting up, I knew we were not keeping below 10,000 feet, as we should have been, because we had no pressurization. It would take twenty minutes for a cigarette to burn completely. Maybe the crew was sneaking some oxygen from their mask system in the cockpit. I hoped so. This was the roughest flight I have ever been on, before or after. We were all glad when we finally broke out into the sunshine and smooth air. And very glad to arrive in Viet Nam so we could get off the smelly plane.

The feeling of being happy to be off the plane did not last long since we were wilting rapidly in the heat; 115° Fahrenheit, which we could tell from the huge thermometer over a hangar door. We, of course, then met the next group of paper pushers from the Wing with the rubber stamps on their desks. They must clone these guys. They look the same, sound the same, and have pretty consistent attitudes. Ron was soon assigned to and on his way to VMO-2, a few miles away at Marble Mountain. John and I were assigned to VMO-6 which required a flight for the fifty miles to Chu Lai, and there was nothing available until the next day. The next day turned out to be the next night. We got to Chu Lai at about ten or eleven and managed to bum a ride in a jeep the mile or so to our new home in Ky Ha, where VMO-6 was located. When we got to the administration hut, there was, of course, nobody around so we just lay down on the ground right outside the door and, exhausted, fell right to sleep. So, on our third day in country, John and I got to work with the last group of paper pushers and were now officially the squadron's newest FNGs (common Marine Corps adjective, New Guy-you figure it out.) We were now all set to begin our new jobs.

Learning Under Fire

When I arrived in Vietnam on 6/6/66, I was one of the early crop of replacements assigned to VMO-6 (code name Klondike). The Marines we were replacing had arrived via ship on 9/1/1965 as a complete squadron from California. They had all trained and been working together a long time. But they would also soon be heading home, starting in July, and would all be gone by September. They were all experienced and had well-defined leadership roles. In June there was not much of a plan about how we replacements were going to make the transition and gain the skills to fill their shoes. Well, I can tell you how my training and transition began. It was like drinking from a fire hose.

The next morning, my third day in VMO-6, I started the process of signing in, getting a bunk, flight gear, side arm etc., and, of course, the endless filling-out of forms, a process that took two to three days. The next step was to fly co-pilot with the experienced pilots to learn the ropes and how the radio systems, frequencies, contacts, call signs, etc., worked so we could help to manage one of a VMO squadron's primary missions, coordinating the troops on the ground, artillery, naval gun fire, attack jets, and troop and cargo helicopter transports and our own direct machine gun and rocket fire support. All of this while, of course, you had to be flying the bird. A VMO UH-1E pilot was always very busy.

After a few of these flights over the next four to five days, I was assigned to be the co-pilot for the medevac gun escort. This was twenty-four-hour stand-by duty. We stayed in the ready room shack, including sleeping there, ready to go at a moment's notice. It was about one o'clock on the morning of June 16th, just one hour into my tenth day in country and a week in squadron, when we were awaken to learn that a recon team had called for an emergency medevac. I ran out on the flight line to meet the crew chief and gunner, got into the left seat, and started the bird, getting all the systems up and running. The pilot, Jim Perryman, remained in the ready room to record all the call signs and frequencies and to plot out the course and distance to the team's location coordinates so we could use the TACAN (TACtical Air Navigation) system to guide us. This was done on an entire wall in the ready room that had the charts for our area of operation glued on it and a big string anchored where the TACAN transmitter was located. There were also a compass rose under the center of the string and a mileage ruler to measure the length of the string needed to reach the location. By locating the coordinates on the map and putting the string onto it, we could determine the radial and the distance from the TACAN to get the fix; for example 22.3 miles on the 293 degree radial. We could then fly directly to the site with no time wasted. It was simple but very quick and accurate.

Jim came running and strapped into the right seat, taxied to the runway, and took off. He made contact with the H-34 that was to be the pickup, that was taking off from the parallel runway, and we proceeded together to help the team. There was no moon out and it was as black as ink. Jim called the recon team, code name Carnival Time, on the assigned FM frequency and we heard a soft, whispered response. Jim knew right away that this was a very bad sign. When they are whispering to you, the VC (Viet Cong) are right there on top of them and they don't want them to hear the radio. If they do, it will make the operator a target and draw fire. We soon learned from the whispering voice that there were eighteen men in the team, pinned down in a bomb crater. They were completely surrounded and had been under attack for some hours. They had two or three KIA (killed in action) and most of the rest were WIA (wounded in action) to some degree. The whisperer (who I later learned was Gunnery Sergeant Jimmie Howard) told us there was no way we could get in to take them out since there were too many enemy. He asked if we could get him air support and some light. Jim told him we would do everything we could to help them out. Jim then asked me to take over flying the aircraft and communicating with the team on the FM so he could use the VHF radio to organize the effort to bring help. So now Jim and I communicated on our intercom, where he kept me informed of what was happening to bring help and I kept him informed about what was happening on the ground.

Jim sent the H-34 home. They wouldn't be needed for a while. Jim got a "Spooky," which was an old R-4 fixed wing transport, to come out and start dropping flares and keeping the area lit. It was so dark that before Spooky arrived we kept losing our bearings as we circled and had to ask the team to give us a quick blink of their flashlight to relocate them.

Even before the flares began, the first of many pairs of jets arrived, ready to lay down the wrath of hell as soon as they could see where we wanted them to put it.

And thus the long night began. Jim, cool, calm, experienced, and in charge, brought a sense of hope to the team on the ground and order out of chaos with those in the air and back on the bases who were doing their jobs to save the team. What was happening at this time was what this war was all about to those of us who were fighting it. Not for glory, not for patriotism, but for our unfaltering commitment to each other.

The whispering did not last after the flares began to drop. Not only did we get to see the team, we also saw that there were dozens and dozens of VC all around the bomb crater, both dead and alive. With the light the VC could also see the team, and the firefight broke out again in earnest. Now the Gunny was shouting to be heard over the gunfire and grenade explosions. We ran some rocket and 30-caliber fire, but air strikes were what was needed.

The Gunny told us exactly where to put air strikes and Jim called them in. "To the east of the crater, fifty yards, come in on a heading of 030° and pull out right. I will fire a willie peter rocket (white phosphorous which produces white smoke), for your mark. We are running you in real close so make a pass and hold your drop so I know you have it right. I repeat: do not drop on your first pass. Acknowledge." "Roger, no drop on this pass," they radioed back. Jim replied, "You are cleared cold; repeat, cold."

I let the team know what was going to happen and then all of a sudden, for the first time in my life, I heard the thunder of the jets going by and pulling up. Gunny Howard called, "That's it, that's it, let'em have it." I told Jim and he made the call, "You are cleared hot." Again I heard the roaring thunder of the jets followed by the 500 lb bombs exploding. What does that sound like when you are only fifty yards away, squeezing yourself onto the ground as flat as a pancake? I cannot imagine. It shook us even that far away and high above. This process went on until we were nearly out of fuel and relieved on station by Captain John Shields and his crew sent from VMO-6. We raced back to an outlying fuel bladder, shut down, checked the bird, walked around for a few minutes while the crew refueled, and back we went, continuing this tag team approach for the rest of the night. After getting back we were briefed by Captain Shields and we got back on the radios to take control, now that we were up to speed on what was happening on the ground and in the air. In the middle of one of my transmissions with Gunny Howard, he gave out a yelp and said, "Shit, I won't be sitting down for awhile. They just hit me again, right in the ass."

While this process continued, there was another KIA and more WIA. Before it was over, there were six KIA and all but one was WIA. But that team was hanging on. We were helping, but those guys on the ground were unbelievable. They never quit and the VC bodies kept piling up all around them. The VC were not quitting either. We learned later that this was a battalion of trainees on a sort of graduation mission.

After two to three more rotations with Captain Shields, we took over again. The work back at the bases was coming together and the sun was finally starting to let us see. The bomb crater where the team was situated was on the corner of a U-shaped ridge that ran about a mile on each side. A platoon of Marines was being inserted on the other corner of the ridge, where there was a spot that would allow the transports to land. The Marines were running the mile along the connecting ridge top to reinforce the team in the crater. Major Goodsell, the commanding officer of VMO-6, and his co-pilot Steve Butler arrived to add more gunbird support. Additional transports were also coming to help extract the team and the reinforcements after they took control and beat back the VC. The tide of battle was starting to swing in Carnival Time's favor, and hope and morale were rising along with the sun.

Upon Major Goodsell's arrival, Jim briefed him on the present status and passed him command of the flight. We fell back into the wingman position. Major Goodsell then proceeded to fly over the team's position in the crater to determine how to best direct the assault of the reinforcements, continuing air strikes and our own thirty-caliber machine gun and rocket fire. From our position 100-200 feet behind, we saw their bird do a bump and a jog, then quickly pull up and right. Immediately we began to receive fire. I will never forget the rhythmic pah-pah-pah sound of that BAR automatic rifle with the rounds tearing up through the center of the cockpit, blowing out all the communication and navigation gear located in the console between Jim and me. Black plastic and radio parts flew everywhere, but not one piece hurt any of us. Jim immediately pulled up and turned to follow the other bird. We had no idea what their status was since, of course, our radios were out, but we had full power and control. As we followed them on a course back toward Ky Ha, it was obvious that they were not able to maintain altitude. They were coming down slowly although maintaining good speed and stable flight.

They came to a clean, controlled landing in a field with Jim and me landing about fifty yards to their right. The crew chief and I immediately leapt out and ran to the other bird. I pulled open the right side door to find Major Goodsell slumped in his seat belts and unresponsive. I freed his belts and put him on my shoulder and started running back to our bird along with our crew chief, Steve Butler and their two crew members. About half way there we saw a local running full speed at us from a hutch at the edge of the paddy. I loaded the Major into the back as the other crew leapt in behind in a big pile. As I climbed back into my seat I was yelling at Jim to "Go, Go, Go," since he couldn't see the local closing in on us fast from behind. As we were lifting off I looked back to see the local throw a satchel charge into the downed bird and run like hell away. In about thirty seconds the charge went off and just blew the bird into a big fireball. For months afterward when flying over the spot you could see about two feet of each rotor blade unburned and the green vegetation slowly growing over the blackened spot.

Thankfully we had burned enough fuel and spent enough ammunition that we could lift off with the huge load we were carrying. The crew in the back soon determined that Major Goodsell was dead. He had a huge wound in the femoral artery and had bled so rapidly that there never was any hope of saving him.

Everything after that is pretty much a blank for me until at about 9-10 AM when all the details and paperwork had been attended to. I sat with Perryman, Butler, Shields and a few others in their hutch. I barely knew any of these men and probably had only said, "Hello, sir," to Major Goodsell once. I was so new to Viet Nam I had no frame of reference to judge the magnitude of my experience over the preceding eight to ten hours. I was a stranger in their midst for all intents and purposes, just another FNG. I watched from the emotional sidelines as these very good friends mourned the horror and loss of one of their own. This, the most tragic day the squadron had experienced since they had been together and had begun to fight in Viet Nam so many months ago, was my first, and at that time, only, experience I had had in battle.

The next day we were off the schedule so I took the opportunity to go to the hospital in Chu Lai to see Gunny Howard. We had had the opportunity to share a pretty horrific night. Me in the relatively safe perch high above the battle, he eyeball to eyeball with his men, who were dead and wounded, and the enemy, who were continually trying to overrun them; yet we had been connected and by more than just a radio. It was quite a meeting. We shook hands as he lay on his stomach to keep off his wounded ass. There was very little said since we both knew the whole story. He did tell me that his hair was turning white almost overnight, just like Simon Peter in the Bible. Gunnery Sergeant, (later to become Sergeant Major) Jimmie Howard was awarded the Medal of Honor, and his Carnival Time team was awarded four Silver Stars and two Navy Crosses for their actions that night. Jim Perryman and John Shields were awarded Silver Stars, as well. The night will only be forgotten when those of us who lived it pass on. Jimmie Howard, who resided in California, died a number of years ago from cancer. I do not know the status of the rest of Carnival Time.

There is no doubt in my mind that this tragedy is what started me on the way to learning the skills that helped me not only survive but to also be able to provide help for so many during the rest of my tour. The old guard provided many of us FNGs the skills we needed so that we could continue the tradition of getting the job done to the very high standards they had set. It was wasn't long before we were no longer the FNGs, but were the old salts as they had left and now the job was up to us.

GYSGT Jimmie Howard

Klondike Playboy

A few days after Major Goodsell was killed in the Jimmie Howard action, the squadron was back at it in full force. I was fortunate to be accepted into the group that the short time flight leaders like Perryman, Shields, Huffcut, Pettigrew, Purcell and others took under their wings to teach the lessons they had learned. They took us as their co-pilots and let us run the show, then as pilots on their wing and again let us run the show. I am sure it was hard for them to turn over the reins, but they knew we wouldn't be able to carry on if they didn't.

It is from this group that I, and some others, received the designation "Playboy." Being a Klondike Playboy and accepting the responsibility it brought with it helped to lift me to be able to become the best I could be—pilot, problem solver and decision maker. Solving problems and making tough decisions are skills that have helped me throughout the rest of my life.

Let me explain what the "Playboy" designation is and then how it was used and why it was needed.

A Playboy was the call sign for a Tactical Air Coordinator Airborne (TACA) and was recognized throughout the squadron, the group and the wing. The troops on the ground, especially the recon teams, knew to call on us. Even the Army Special Forces Studies and Observation

Group (SOG) used to call on Playboys to lead their operations against the Ho Chi Minh trail on the other side of borders to the West and North that were not to be divulged. The jet pilots knew to come under the Playboys' command and follow their instructions. Two attack jets were kept on the end of the runway at Chu Lai and could be in the air in less than five minutes, if a Playboy called to DASC (Direct Air Support Center) for them. When we needed more, DASC would send them from Chu Lai, Da Nang, the aircraft carriers, and even from the Air Force in Thailand. When a Playboy said it was needed, they could change the status of a "no fire zone" to "free fire." Playboys were given a huge amount of responsibility and were treated with respect because of the work they did. Their role was not unlike that of the captains of the sixteenth and seventeenth century schooners that were part of the British Navy fleets. These schooners were often skippered by young lieutenants whose mission as fleet messengers often kept them away from hierarchy and direct supervision and often led to wild adventures. They were here, there, and the other place, and getting into all kinds of situations. They weren't much when it came to "working by the book" but were often requested for the tough and challenging problems because those in control knew they were the men to call on when they had to get the job done. Just like the schooner skippers before them, Playboys spent many, many days away from their squadrons and free of their day to day direction, living with the SOG teams, temporarily attached to other squadrons and task force operation commands throughout both the I Corps and II Corps, which were the two most northern US military zones of South Viet Nam.

When Playboys were on the scene, they coordinated the transports, medevac, artillery, and naval gunfire, made the decisions about when and how to do insertions and extractions, and acted as eyes in the sky helping direct the movements of the troops on the ground. They were called on to make some of the hardest decisions. Like the call that a zone was too hot to land and that we weren't going to be able to get the troops on the ground out of there at that time. We made mistakes but learned to accept the fact that we weren't perfect and didn't let the fear of failure hold us back from doing what needed doing, day after day.

Playboys were not everywhere all the time, and they were only involved in some of the thousands of actions where every pilot was asked to make these same kinds of decisions on his own. But if a Playboy was available, usually everyone was glad to see him. Many times they would hear a call on the Guard channel "Is there a Playboy in the area? We need help. Please come up on channel XYZ."

During their tours in Viet Nam, the pilots of VMO-6 with the special skills to do this critical and complex mission floated to the surface and were recognized. These skills did not always correspond to one's military rank. As you can imagine, this meant that when operations officers needed to assign the best person to be the plane's pilot (right seat) and to designate who was to be the flight's leader making the decisions during critical missions, a lot of sticky issues arose. First and foremost their task was to maximize the odds that the missions would be accomplished while keeping the crews

111

and planes as safe as possible. A lot was riding on their choices. They needed to assure that the best person was assigned to the job, even if he wasn't the one with the highest rank. This is the reason the Playboy designation was conceived. The "powers that be," and no one ever seemed to know who exactly they were, periodically designated a new Playboy. It was very much like the system back in Pensacola on the academy yawls that let a 21 year old MARCAD become a skipper even though he may have had the lowest military rank on board. This below-the-surface system was in place before I arrived, and I only understood its real significance when the old guard starting going home and I, a second lieutenant, started being assigned the right seat and acting as the flight leader because I had been made a Playboy with all the associated authority. There were some captains and many majors that didn't understand what was going on and would complain. But they got the picture soon enough. The co-pilots, crew chiefs and gunners understood. They had their lives on the line and damn sure wanted the best chance to get their butts home in one piece. If you don't think they had a big effect on which pilots they flew with, you don't understand the Marine Corps. I am sure they had a hand through the backdoor to the "powers that be."

I know it is true for me, and I think for the other Playboys as well, that the respect and recognition we were afforded during our time in Viet Nam was a highlight in our lives. I have often said that the things I was able to do as a Playboy allowed me hundreds of opportunities to do more good for more people in a day than most are able to do in a lifetime. What a privilege it was to be a Playboy.

Playboy Designation

SQUADRON TAC(A) PATCH, GIVEN TO
PILOTS DESIGNATED AS TACTICAL AIR
CONTROLLERS AIRBORNE.

Playboy Patch

Oops! Suit

Thankfully I was not responsible for every off the wall thing that happened in the I-Corps of Viet Nam. In this particular tale I was not completely out of the loop but was far from the center of the real action. As July and August of 1966 continued to bear down on us with temperatures over 100° day after day, we kept trying to find new ways to minimize our discomfort. One approach was to wear fewer clothes. This process began to slowly creep into what we wore when flying. I think it started with not wearing our gloves, which would become a sticky glob of wet, smelly leather that got so slippery, it was as if your hand was greased. Then next it was taking your arms out of your flight suit and tying it around your waist. I will admit I did fly a couple of hops in as little as shorts, tee shirt, flip-fops, and earphones instead of a helmet.

This disregard for appropriate flight gear was more or less prevalent through all the squadrons at Ky Ha at the time we got a new Group CO (Commanding Officer). When he had been there just a few days and realized the extent of the issue about flight gear, he went ballistic. Quite appropriately, I will have to admit. All that gear was supposed to be worn for a reason, and the safety issues and the effect it could have on others made our not wearing it irresponsible.

So the order came swiftly down the chain of command to all of us that any deviation from proper clothing and equipment while flying would be dealt with severely. There was not much grumbling since we all knew it was the right thing to do and immediately the problem was gone.

It was about three days later and the new CO was leaving his office to go to lunch. Please note that his office was just to the north of the approach to the north runway, so the H-34s and H-46s that used the north end would be less than fifty feet high and fifty feet south of his doorway. As he looked up at the H-34 going by that day, he was flabbergasted to see that the co-pilot was flying with no shirt to cover his arms and chest. He went roaring back into his office, called the squadron CO of the offending pilot, and told him "Get that SOB right now and bring his sorry butt to my office immediately."

This was not a pleasant call for the squadron CO, who slammed down the phone and went immediately out onto the flight line and over to the bird, which was just shutting down. He walked around to the co-pilot's side just in time to see him climbing down the side of the bird. To his utter amazement, not only was he not wearing a shirt, he was wearing nothing at all except his helmet, boots and chest armor. This gave him a fine view of the pilot's butt, and when the pilot had reached the ground and turned around, the two of them were staring at each other with mouths hanging open and speechless. Finally the CO sputtered, "What the hell is going on? Why are you naked?"

"Sorry sir, I couldn't help it," was the incredible answer. His story went like this. He was returning from a re-supply mission when he had to go and go then, not an uncommon occurrence in Viet Nam. There was no waiting; what was inside wanted out and was threatening an explosive escape at any moment. There appeared to be only one possible solution, which was to land in an open field, right then, and let the growling beast free. So down they went. He climbed out with speed and dexterity not often seen, tore off his chest armor, unzipped his flight suit, shrugged it off his shoulders, and squatted just as the monster got loose. Ah, relief.

Oops, he had a problem. His flight suit had not gotten out of the line of fire and now held the remains of the defeated beast. What else could he do but, as carefully as possible, step out of the legs of the flight suit? He certainly couldn't put it back on. He then rolled it up and, I am sure, much to the delight of the crew chief put it into the cargo bay with him. He walked back around to the front of the bird and climbed back up to take his station and they took off and came home. His bad luck was obviously still in full force since his timing coordinated so well with the Colonel's desire to eat lunch. His story did take the wind out of the anger about disobeying orders, and since the powers were unable to come up with any possible appropriate response, the issue just evaporated. But it was the last of the under-dressed pilot incidents at Ky Ha.

Every day life in Ky Ha

Doing Laundry

The Doc and Dentist Saving Their Office During a
Monsoon Rain

More information and photos at

Maintenance Test Hop

All flight officers, in addition to their job as pilots, are also assigned to another job in the squadron. Some are very important such as commanding officer, operations officer, maintenance officer, etc. Other assignments are considerably less important. My other job assignment was so unimportant I never even knew what it was. I probably did have one that was noted somewhere on a personnel roster in the back of a file drawer somewhere. You can bet I never asked about it since it could have led to trouble such as having to actually do some work. Since I didn't know what my other job was, neither did anyone else. This worked out great for me, since it meant that there was never any reason for me not to be flying. It also meant that, when one or two birds were assigned to go off for a couple of days, a week, and even one time for over a month to support operations out of our area, I was usually on the list to go. This was fine with me, since, when I was away on these assignments; there was no rank above me telling me how to do things. I got my mission assignments and it was then up to me to get the job done in the most effective and efficient way. I was the skipper, even if I only had one or two birds to be the skipper of.

Of course I was not away from the squadron all the time, nor were there missions to be flown every day. Sometimes we were grounded due to weather and sometimes there was just not much action that needed our assistance. Therefore, those who had jobs at the approximate level of importance of mine could read, do laundry, cut their hair, etc. But I often hung around the ready room so that, if a mission did get called in, I would be right there and ready to take it. One ready room activity that was almost always under way was a game of Acey Ducey, a backgammon variation that was found in every naval aviator ready room I was ever in. The winner got to keep his place at the board and face the next challenger, which meant that ninety percent of the time I was either waiting my turn in line to play or was the challenger who got to play and then got back into line again. Often that meant I played against Barney Ross, who seemed to be the luckiest player in the squadron. He, of course, continually insisted that it was skill that made him the winner so often, but I don't know anyone who ever agreed with him on that point.

One day while I was reading in the ready room, KD Waters, a senior captain, came and yelled "Hey, Boden, get your ass over here. I got something I want you to do for me." KD's "other" job was maintenance officer, which was a very big and important job. He probably had more than half our men working for him, and the success of the entire squadron was always riding on his shoulders, since without birds ready to fly, the squadron was of no use. KD had arrived about four months before me, was an ex-jet jockey, and had learned his lessons well in the UH-1E. He was a very good pilot and knew the ins and outs of a Playboy's job calling the jets because he had been there and done that. He taught me a lot when I had the privilege of being his co-pilot as I first started flying in country. He usually had a scowl and his eyes could bore right through you, telling the world he didn't take excuses and you were expected to do your job and do it right. Once he decided you could hold up your end of the stick, he relaxed around you and was funny as hell.

I, of course, leapt right up and followed him out the door into the maintenance shack. "This is Corporal Corning. He needs you to help him track the rotor blades on his bird. He knows what he is doing, so you do whatever he tells you he needs you to do," he said and walked away. Corning didn't hesitate a second and said, "My bird is already pushed out onto the other side of the field and is ready. I need you to start it, and then, when you are at 6,600 rpm, hold the cyclic neutral and perfectly still so I can get the marks on the stick. When I am done, I will signal you to shut down so we can make adjustments; any questions?" "Not now. I'll get my flight gear out of the ready room and meet you at the bird," I said. "You won't need flight gear." he replied. "Just turn it up, not fly it; that's all you want me to do?" I asked. "Yes, sir," was his answer. I had no idea what this was all about, but KD had said to do whatever Corning said so I followed him out to his bird, climbed in, started up, and gave him the nod when I was at 6,600 rpm, neutral load, and had the cyclic held firmly. Corning walked over alongside the left skid and picked up a pole about ten feet long, with a big bunch of masking tape wrapped around the top three feet of it. I couldn't believe my eyes as he took the pole about six feet in front of the windshield, put the unwrapped end on the ground, and then brought the wrapped end up until the top was above and just outside the rotor plane.

121

For a minute I thought he must have been trying to kill himself. KD trusted him and said he knew what he was doing so I watched in disbelief as ever so slowly and gently he brought the stick closer and closer to the blades until I heard zip, zip, and he moved the stick away and laid it on the ground and signaled me to shut down.

As soon as I got everything shut down and the rotor brake brought the blades to a full stop, I climbed out to find out what this was all about. I am not going to give you a lesson on blade balancing except to say that red and green grease pencils were used to mark the tabs on the end of each blade. When the tabs cut through the masking tape on the pole you could see which blade was high and which was low and by how much. Using this scientific approach, they climbed up onto the rotor head, adjusted nuts, and added or removed some weight. Then the process was done again and again, sometimes five or six times, with new masking tape covering the old mark until there was only one cut with both red and green color on it.

This was my introduction and lesson one in becoming a maintenance check pilot (PMIP). Tracking rotors was only one part of doing maintenance checks, but the longest and surely the most boring part. Becoming a check pilot made me a lot safer since I had to learn what had been done to each bird, what to look for in preflight, and the procedures to follow in flight to confirm it would operate to proper specifications. And, by the way, the stick got snatched out of a crewman's hands and thrown for a loop only once in all the times I saw it done, and nobody was hurt.

One hot afternoon, maintenance found me to fly a comprehensive check on a bird that had been down for more than a month waiting for a part we didn't have. As sometimes happened, it had turned into a spare parts supply source to keep other birds in the air. Parts were almost always a problem. After a while, however, a bird that was being reported as down too long began to get the attention of the paper pushers at the Air Group headquarters and it had to get back into the air. This bird would require many system checks since it had been stripped down to her skin and frame and rebuilt.

The crew chief and I went over her with a fine-toothed comb during preflight and all looked good to go. We had a clerk-admin type going with us to log flight hours. He knew that riding maintenance check flights for the time needed to collect flight pay was a hell of a lot safer than flying as a gunner and getting shot at. Well, not this day, as we were all soon to learn. We took off and I climbed to 3,000 feet. This was higher than I needed to go, but going to that altitude was like going into an air-conditioned room because the temperature was much cooler than the 100 plus degrees on the flight line that day.

I began the long list of tests as the crew chief relaxed and the passenger read his book. I had been at it about fifteen to twenty minutes when I thought I got a quick whiff of smoke. I asked if either of them smelled anything and got a negative. So I continued with the procedures. It wasn't two minutes later and the crew chief was yelling "smoke, smoke!" so I turned around to look and there definitely was smoke. I immediately went into an auto rotation and started down as fast as I could go and still keep the rotor rpm under control. I called Ky Ha tower and told them I had smoke but was not declaring an emergency. I then asked them to hold all traffic on the south runway and for clearance to land downwind to the west. They cleared me and made the calls to keep everybody out of the pattern and from taxiing. All was going well and the smoke didn't seem to be getting any worse so the only thing I had to work on was being absolutely cool and making sure my crew and those on the ground stayed that way, too. As I was going through 1,000 feet, the tower called. "Go ahead, Ky Ha," I radioed back. "You have flames about ten feet high coming out of your rotor head area," they reported. So, remembering that sounding cool was of primary importance, I recalled an old Army Air Corps song and responded, "Well, if that's the case, 'You'd Better Get the Crash Crew, and Get'em On the Run,'" a line from a song of the same title. The bird was behaving perfectly, all the gauges were in the green, and I was right on track to land at the intersection of the runway and the taxiway, which gave me the largest amount of room for error. I didn't know what was causing the fire and, since I was in an auto rotation, I put every switch in the off position and shut down the engine so there would be no fuel added to the problem. I came into my flare, turning to face the taxiway, and set her down like a feather. I reached up to pull the rotor brake handle just as the crash truck came roaring down the taxiway right on time. They had a man sitting on top holding the handles of the foam gun ready to lay it on us. Oops, they were coming a little too fast and so, when they got finally stopped, the foam gun was inside the rotor's diameter and—whap!—the rotor blade hit it. The bird spun ninety degrees left with the rotor's blade still hard against the foam gun and about six inches from the guy on top with his hands still on the handles. It took us about all of one second to recover our wits and get the hell out and away from the bird. The crew chief was the hero that day. He didn't run; he was ready and had our fire extinguisher in his hands right after I started the descent. When he jumped out after our rude welcome, he crawled under the bird and shot the extinguisher up the "Hell Hole" (an opening that went up all the way around the rotor shaft). He had the fire out in less than a minute. When the emergency was over, we realized everybody in the crash truck was still sitting there with frozen looks of horror on their faces.

It turned out that the rotor brake, one of the items replaced, had the brake pads dragging just lightly enough to finally heat up and start the fire. You couldn't see the brake pads in the preflight so there was no way to find that. It was the crash crew's first real emergency call in more than the year since they had arrived in Ky Ha. They now had an enviable record. One time out and one fire successfully extinguished. It was too bad they weren't the ones that put it out, and, oh, yeah, they were also sorry about the accident they caused.

To this day the story brings tears to KD's eyes thinking about all the paperwork and having to start all over rebuilding the bird back again from skin and bones.

Rotor Adjust Pole In Use
(notice the aiming cross hairs on the windshield)

A Long Day — Almost Too Long

It was early fall and VMO-6 was still desperately short of pilots but still filling mission requests without excuses by getting the birds in the air with every trick we could think up. The rulebook said a UH-1E could be flown with one pilot in the right seat on any flight that didn't involve direct contact with the enemy. This rule is the main reason the generals and other VIPs wanted to be flown in a UH-1E. It meant they could sit in the left seat and feel like the very special persons they all knew they were. I am aware of one case where Brigadier General Stiles, whose headquarters were very near Ky Ha had Barney Ross assigned to be his personal pilot and got a considerable amount of flight training while in the left seat and was able to actually take off and land before Barney was rotated back to the States. I think that may have been the end of the General's flying, but he and Barney kept up their relationship for years afterward.

One of the solutions we came up with to help with our pilot shortage was to go recruiting. The other helicopter squadrons were usually very busy so they were not a good source. So I went a little further down the road to the officers club at Chu Lai, the fixed wing base. After a couple of beers it was pretty easy to get the conversation around to being a Playboy and being used to giving orders to jet jockeys. From there it often went to who had the bigger *cojones*—the guy who was high and fast or the guy who was low and slow. Once the conversation got up to a full roar I was able to get in the last word. "If you think you do have what it takes, come fly with me," I would challenge. That always brought a pause to the banter, in which I would say, "How about at eight tomorrow morning? You got what it takes or not?"

I usually had them then. How could a jet jockey's ego ever let him back down? This source of co-pilots made us legal, but everyone knew there was no way they would ever get the bird home if something happened. They were better than one of the recruits that I got to fly with me. I met some swift boat captains at the Chu Lai club one night and they were listening in on my "who has the biggest *cojones*" pitch, when one of them said he'd go. I had thought it would be fun to go out on a swift boat so I made him a deal. I would take him on a mission with me if he would take me on a mission with him. "Consider it done," was the answer. That's how a swift boat captain became a helicopter co-pilot, and how I got a twenty-four hour swift boat ride. I do believe that he pretty much figured he got more than his money's worth and had no more desire to be a co-pilot again.

We slowly began to get more pilots to fill our ranks. I think we actually reached the point in late September or early October when we were working with as few as eight pilots in flight ready status, but we always did what we had to do to get the job done. It was early November when an H-46 driver, Bill Walker, arrived in Ky Ha with a new squadron that had a full complement of pilots. When he heard we were short-handed at VMO-6 he started angling for a transfer. A transfer was going to be complicated and take time, but we could arrange to get him some slots to fly with us, if he was interested. He didn't hesitate a minute.

Operations got a request for a bird to go to Marble Mountain and support Deadlock (our sister squadron, VMO-2). I got the job, happy to get away as always, and Bill was assigned as my co-pilot for his first time in a UH-1E. We hit it off right away and found it easy to work together since we combined teaching and the process of working together, from mission assignment, preflight, procedures, and on and on. I do not remember Deadlock ever coming down and supporting us; there were lots of times one, two or more of our birds were working out of Marble Mountain helping them. One of the reasons for this was that they had a VIP mission that involved a lot more work than was required by the one-star General with whom we flew and who was aware of priorities and did not call on us unless it was necessary. VMO-2, on the other hand, was located near the throne of the Marine leadership for all of Viet Nam. Theirs was a General who knew how to take full advantage of all the benefits due those of someone in such an exalted position. He not only had his own helo-pad at his quarters on his private island in Da Nang Harbor, he also insisted on having a bird there with crew ready to take him, his staff, or his star-studded personal guests to any destination at a moment's notice. And, in case there were more guests than could be safely transported in that bird, he had another on stand-by at the squadron. He was known universally as BDL for Big Dumb Lou. I am sure that actually writing this down and being accountable for it would not be recommended; however, I do not think you will be able to find many of those there at the time that would deny it. Not even Martha.

We got our gear packed, although we didn't know how long we would be away, and took off for Marble Mountain. We flew a couple of missions for them that day and then were sent up to Phu Bai, a base with a small airstrip south of Hue City. They had a small group of H-46s covering the whole area from the Hai Van pass to the DMZ (Demilitarized Zone between North and South Viet Nam). There were no gun birds with them. The next morning Bill and I got our first mission to cover a medevac to the east near the coast. We located the ground troops, who told us they were taking fire from their east in a tree line. I set up to put fire into that area while the H-46 stood by. Pulling up from our first run we started taking fire, and immediately Bill took a round in his left calf. I called to the Medevac bird and the troops on the ground to inform them my co-pilot was wounded and we had to abort the medevac. I found what looked like a secure and open field to land along with the H-46 so they could take Bill. They had the corpsman aboard and Bill was bleeding very badly and needed attention immediately. As soon as I landed, Bill opened his own door, unstrapped, got out, and started hopping on one leg to get out from under the rotor before the corpsman and crew chief of the H-46 could get to him. They got him in the bird and flew him to the hospital ship *Repose* that was just off the coast. That was the last I saw or heard of Bill Walker until I got a call twenty-five years later. I answered my phone in my office and a voice said to me, "Do you remember where you were and what you were doing on November 4th, twenty-five years ago?"

and I immediately answered, "Yes, I do. I had a co-pilot wounded that day and you must be him." Time could separate us but the connection was never broken. I met with his family and him at a reunion the next year. When he introduced me as being with him when he was wounded, his family said to him, "Well, maybe it's time you finally told us the story." In all those years, with all that he had to face, telling the story was something he hadn't wanted to do. He said, "John, why don't you start?" So I was able to be his co-pilot as he relived it again with his family. I was honored to be included.

The longest day was now well under way. The Crew chief, gunner and I flew back to Phu Bai. The post-flight inspection showed that the rounds that had hit us had done no damage to the bird beyond adding some extra ventilation ports, so we were ready to take missions. While the crew had the awful job of cleaning the plane, and it was not pretty, and getting the bird ready to go again, I went to see if I could find a co-pilot. "Sorry, we can't help you with that, but the H-46 is back from the *Repose* and ready to restart the original mission," they responded. It was obvious what they were asking so I went back to my bird and asked my crew if they were willing to go with me as solo pilot. No hesitation from them so we launched. They got the original medevac out and we didn't take any more fire. As soon as we were done, the DASC contacted me with another mission. This went on, mission after mission after mission. We ate C-rations and took leaks while we refueled. It was dark now and the DASC had yet another mission. Two very badly wounded ARVN (Army of the Republic of Viet Nam) soldiers, near the DMZ needed a medevac to the *Repose*. I had more than eleven hours in the air at that point, but, what the hell. I got the coordinates and headed out to get them. We were a gun bird, remember, but I guess there was nobody else. We were light enough by then to take them since we had shot our rockets and burned fuel.

When we got them on board and we were airborne, the crew chief told me that one of them was really bad and that he was going to start mouth to mouth to help him breathe. I headed for the *Repose*, climbing to 3,000 feet to avoid enemy fire. In about fifteen minutes we were over the *Repose*. She was lit up and easy to see all the way out. I called for landing and began my descent, making circles around the ship. At one point I looked back to check on how the crew chief was doing and when I looked back out, holy crap, where did the *Repose* go?! I was confused and befuddled when the crew chief yelled, "Pull up, pull up, pull up." I immediately responded with power and cyclic and then saw the green navigation light reflecting in the water not five feet below. If there was a medal for saving a stupid pilot's ass, as well as all those of the others on board, including his own, he deserved it. Giving mouth to mouth and still staying alert to what was going on around him was as good as it gets. And I will have to admit I cannot even remember who he was. If you're out there, please let me know who you are.

One small inattention on my part—that was all it took for me to bring six souls to the edge of death. What had happened was that, when I took my eyes off flying to look at the crew chief, the *Repose*, as was the correct procedure, had shut down all her lights except the low level lights around the landing pad. And I had gotten lower than the deck and so I saw no lights at all and that left me with nothing to orient on.

We got aboard, transferred the ARVNs, and I launched, heading back for the barn at Phu Bai. Would you believe I got another call? This one was to pick up a VIP and take him to Phu Bai with us. It was going to take an additional thirty minutes and another takeoff and landing. I declined. They were not happy; the VIP was not happy, but frankly, my dear, I didn't give a damn. I was no longer a safe pilot and I was getting us home and onto the ground the fastest way possible.

When I was signing in at the operations desk, I got a message to see their CO. I told them that I would see him in the morning because I was going to bed then. The next morning, when I reported in as ordered, I got my ass chewed up one side and down the other, not for damn near killing five people, but for not picking up some General. It ended with me being ordered to get my ass, my crew and my bird to hell out of Phu Bai. No problem with that order, and the three of us were gone in a flash.

As soon as I got back to Ky Ha and signed in the bird, I went to see the skipper. He had already heard the story and calmly asked me to sit down and tell him what had happened. When I was through, the only thing he had to say, was, "Will you stop flying sooner next time?" "Yes, sir," I responded and meant it. Then he commented, "You made the right choice when you refused the mission." That was it. The next day I learned he put me up for

R&R in Hawaii. I heard him, I heard him loud and clear and I am also sure he had to take some ass chewing of his own on my part.

Hue Before Tet Offensive

Man and Machine

I did not fly a plane. I strapped a machine on to me and we became a bird. Doing things the machine could not do without me, and things I could not do without the machine. We became one and did it together. I had to learn about and listen to the machine, respecting her for all that she could do, while the machine learned to respect me and gave back all that she had to give. When a machine reflects her lights off the surface of the water in the black of night so your crewman can see it and warn you, she was certainly more than just a machine when she saved all our lives.

VIP Flights

It was a cold and rainy day with the ceiling at under 300 feet and nothing was getting off the ground. VMO-6 had a mission request from the ROK (Republic of Korea) Marines who were set up and operating from a base about twenty miles south of Chu Lai. It had come in the night before, calling for a pickup of their commanding General at 8 AM to fly him to a meeting in Chu Lai. Operations had this and all the other requests sitting in a pile waiting for the weather to break. At about 9 AM a call came in to say the General was waiting and wanted to get picked up immediately. The weather issues were explained to them again. Then about every half hour we got another call and soon there was pressure being applied from other higher up sources to go pick up this ROK General.

At about 11 AM, with some let up in the drizzling rain, I volunteered to go. I was bored hanging around and this would give me something to do. I had worked with the ROKs a number of times before and knew where they wanted us to land in their headquarters. I launched and flew right down Highway One (the main road from the DMZ to the Mekong Delta) at tree top level so that, by the time anyone on the ground figured out a helicopter was coming, we would have blown right by before they could do anything to get organized and take a shot at us.

136

I landed on the ROK LZ (Landing Zone), and the General and his staff were there ready to go. When the crew chief jumped out to help them aboard he told me on the intercom that he had noticed we had picked up a few miscellaneous leaves and small branches that were still on the skids. As he was helping the General into the left seat and the staff was climbing into the back, he and I also realized that the ROKs had noticed the leaves and branches. We, of course, could not understand what they were saying, but all the pointing and re-checking and their excited, animated voices said it all. I asked the crew chief over the intercom to remove any material we may have accumulated on the skids, which he did in a most methodical way. While he was doing this, we continued our conversation about how excited the ROKs seemed to be while we both struggled to keep from breaking out laughing.

When he was done, he got aboard and then fitted the General and his English-speaking aide, who was in the jump seat behind and between the pilot's seats, with headsets so they could hear the radio transmissions and use the intercom to talk with me. I welcomed them aboard and shook hands with them both. Of course I mentioned not a word about the natural decorations that the crew chief had just removed from the skids. I did, however, explain the extent of the poor weather conditions and apologized for having to delay our arrival due to safety concerns. I then explained to them that the safest way to reach Chu Lai for their meeting was to go back the same way I had gotten there and then explained the low level over Highway One plan and the reason why it was the best strategy to avoid enemy fire

137

since the 300 foot ceiling prevented us from going high enough to be above the reach of small arms fire. As the aide was translating, I lifted off and started west for the highway. We had an uneventful ride north, only touching a few treetops here and there. The ROKs seemed to be getting their money's worth, however. Again we couldn't understand them, but they all seemed to be agreeing that getting shot at was probably not going to happen.

We landed in Chu Lai, discharged our passengers, and shut down to wait for their return when the meeting was over. Well, it wasn't ten minutes and there they were, back again. The aide said the meeting had been canceled so they didn't need to have come anyway. We loaded up and back we went. There seemed to be very little conversation now and I guess that maybe somebody who was smart enough to have canceled the meeting due to weather conditions had made that point to them.

When we landed, the General was all smiles and shaking my hand. The aide said the General was very satisfied with all I had done for his safety and wanted me to join him and his staff for lunch. During lunch I had a minimal amount of conversation since English was a rare commodity. At one point all conversation stopped around the table. I had just put a portion of kimchi onto my chopsticks. I took a bite and thought my head was going to explode. Everyone broke out laughing, in a good-natured way, and the aide provided lots of advice about how to put out the fire. When I could finally breathe again, I laughingly shook my finger at them, which caused another huge laugh around the table. I realized this was a standard rite of passage for their Yankee brethren, and, at a number of meals that I had with them subsequently, they were always very helpful and careful to see I didn't get into any more dietary dilemmas.

And, by the way, any time after that, if we had to delay a mission request from the ROKs due to weather, we never heard another complaint.

John, taken by Y.S. Kim of the ROKMC on 4/67

Boarding Local Boat

Skipper Watching Swift Boat's Smoky Diesels

Under the Influence

D rinking was surely our main process for stress relief. Of course no one had ever heard of "stress relief" or "stressed out" in the sixties; we only had "overworked and tired." When we were overworked and tired we had a few drinks and went to bed. The next day you weren't tired anymore and you hadn't done any work yet, so, of course, you couldn't be overworked. With all the drinking and all the flying I only recall one time when there was less than a minimum of eight hours between bottle and throttle. Hung over, maybe, but drunk, no.

It was about one o'clock in the morning and the rest of my hooch mates and I were fast asleep. We had all been at the club until about an hour before. The operations duty officer came in, flipped on the lights, and started yelling for us all to get up. "What the hell is the matter with you? Garner, get the hell out of here and leave us alone," was the universal response. "Get up! Marble Mountain is under attack and I have to send up two birds to find the mortar position and attack it. Somebody's going."

As we stumbled out of bed he came up to each of us and gave a shove; the four who didn't fall down were picked to go. I was one of the lucky ones and had to get dressed, go down to the ready room, get my gear, and launch for Marble Mountain. By the time we got there, of course, the attack was over and all we could do was land there at

141

the VMO-2 area and go back to bed. The scariest part of this experience was when I woke up in the morning and realized I was with VMO-2 and had no memory of how the hell I had gotten there. It worked out that time, but you can be sure there was no way I was ever going to get talked into doing that again.

Marble Mountain

You Never Know
Where a Mission Will Lead You

On another afternoon, when things were slow and I was up for flying anything, I was bugging the operations duty officer for something to do. It turned out there was a request that nobody could figure out. It involved a drop at the General's landing pad about 500 yards south of Ky Ha with the pickup for twelve passengers from the hospital ship *Repose* at 5 PM. Since this was for twelve passengers, it would require two birds. What the hell was this all about? There was also an accompanying mission for a pickup at the General's landing pad at 8 PM for twelve passengers with the *Repose* as the destination. There had to be something interesting going on here and I wanted in on it. This was not a VIP flight request for the General, but it looked like getting his pilot, Barney Ross, to lead this two bird mission would be a good idea. At 4:45, with our curiosity at the boiling point, I lifted off right behind Barney to fly to the *Repose*, which was anchored a mile or two off the end of our runway and the General's landing pad.

Barney made contact and began his approach. Their landing pad was built up onto the aft section of the ship. It was, of course, an afterthought for this WW II ship whose designers had no need to think about helicopters in her day. It was a nice afternoon with a gentle breeze and only a small sea running.

While we are talking about landing on the *Repose*, let me get side-tracked for a minute and tell you about what it is like to land aboard her when it is blowing forty knots and the seas are running 10-12 feet. In these conditions the *Repose* rides like a hobbyhorse. She dips her bow and then sticks her ass way, way up in the air. Then, of course, the stern falls like a rock when the wave comes out from under her. Because there is no sense in making things easy, let's do this in the pitch dark with a little rain added so the ship's flight deck personnel can better share in the thrill. At night, for landing operations, the ship shuts off all its lights except those around the edge of the landing pad. So you go from seeing what looks like a small town all lit up to suddenly only being able to see what looks like a small black, square hole with some dim lights at the edge, which is the pad where you are going to land.

After being cleared to land and being assured they were ready to get the tie-down chains onto the skids the moment I touched down, I came up to the stern and went into a hover. I started to work at staying level with the landing pad by matching the rise and fall of the stern. After a couple of cycles and at the top of the rise and just as that pause occurred before she fell again, I radioed them I was coming on and jumped onto the pad and rode her down. Once on the deck I immediately dropped the power to get the weight fully onto the skids so the deck crew could get the chains on and locked down without us sliding around the pad or, even worse, over the side. The hardest part of a landing like this, and, thank God, there were only a few, was to keep flying while your heart was in your throat and the seat cushion was puckered all the way up to a full factor of ten. It was much easier to take off but still pretty spectacular. The crew chief was lying on his stomach with his head out the door so he could see all four tie downs and, as we came to the top of the wave, I would signal the air boss to let the chains go. The crew chief verified that we were disconnected and I pulled the collective into my arm pit and up we went just as the ship went down. We're out of there!

Well, back to the story.

Barney lands and the passengers start across the pad with one getting into the left seat and five others into the back with the help of the crew chief. They weren't even half loaded when Barney comes up on the VHF approach frequency and tells me to come up on an FM frequency which he rattled off. I tuned it in and there was Barney. "Boden, you won't believe this but I just picked up six nurses. Female nurses!" We knew there had to be something going on and there sure was. "You're kidding me," I replied. "No, I'm not. I'm lifting off. It's your turn now," he said. So I called for landing, was cleared, went in, touched down, got the chains on, and, lo and behold, here came my passengers. Not only were they nurses; they were in civilian clothes and dressed to the nines. I did have one thorn with my roses. There was a male Lt Commander and it was immediately obvious that he was not happy with whatever was going on. He wanted to get into the left seat but I told him no, which really helped to raise his morale. I motioned for one of the nurses to come around and get in the seat instead. With everybody loaded, the crew chief got a headset for the nurse next to me and I explained to her how to use the intercom button to talk. I then called for takeoff and lifted, turning right to climb up and join in formation with Barney. It was pretty obvious that those girls were thrilled and as excited as fifteen year olds at an Elvis concert. I slid right up into close formation and now the girls from each plane were waving at each other. We only had a mile to go so I needed to work fast to find out what the story was here. The grouchy Lt. Commander was in the jump seat just behind me on the centerline, and he kept tapping me on the shoulder trying to tell me something. I couldn't hear him and could not have cared less anyway. There was not a peep from Barney on the FM so I figured he was busy on the intercom talking to one of his passengers and I'd best be doing the same. "Hi, I'm John. What's your name? Go ahead and push the button right there." "Like this?" she came back. "Yes," I responded. "Hi, John, my name is Peggy Sue", she told me. "Peggy Sue, what is the story here? Where are you all going and why?" I asked. "Oh, we have been invited to a dinner party with the General and his staff," she answered. "A dinner party with the General and his staff? You're kidding me, right?" "No, it's true," she responded. "How would you all like to come to a party with some pilots?" I immediately asked. "That sounds like fun," she said. By this time Barney was already on the General's pad and was unloaded. I made my approach and landed while the Lt. Commander behind me was having a conniption because I hadn't paid any attention to him and was obviously chatting up Peggy Sue. He was yelling that we had better be back there at exactly 8 pm to return them to the ship or he'd have my ass, etc., etc. I don't know what it is about me, but I seem to piss off almost every Major and Lt. Commander I come into contact with, and for no apparent reason. The landing strip at Ky Ha is literally so close to the General's pad that I called for landing to the west while I was still sitting on the pad. I lifted off, making a wide left hand turn and was over the runway. As soon as I taxied, landed and shut down, I beat feet for the ready room as I knew Barney would be telling the story to everyone he could get his hands on and I didn't want to miss out on any of this.

This situation had "opportunity for a Major under-the-radar operation" written all over it. It was not the first time I had seen American women in Viet Nam since I had flown a small group of female Red Cross personnel on a few occasions from one outlying Special Forces outpost to another with about an hour wait in the bird at each post. They would never even say hello to the flight crew. (What do you suppose they were doing?) Anyway, that's another story.

I had made an invitation to come to a party with Marine pilots and Peggy Sue had readily accepted, so we knew we had willing partners in the escapade. But the when, where, how, and the hundreds of paper-pounding field grade officers having to authorize such a party left any future plan with too many insurmountable obstacles. So it was immediately obvious that, if anything was going to come of this, we needed to act right away. We had about two hours left to make this happen, which was plenty of time for a couple of Klondike Playboys. I will leave out the planning process and cut directly to the maneuver, except to say we did need to recruit our flight surgeon to help us out.

At 7:45 PM Barney and I launched and in less than one minute we were sitting one behind the other on the General's pad. We shut down since there seemed to be

147

nobody anywhere around. Barney and I, as well as the crew chiefs, who were fully into the plan at this point, were as excited as little kids with a secret. It was about 8:15 when we finally spotted some vehicles coming up the hill behind the General's quarters, so we started the birds to be fully prepared and ready to go.

In just a few more minutes we saw not only the nurses and their hovering chaperone but also a gaggle of guys in civilian clothes fully intermixed with them. And guess who was in the middle of it? The General himself. It was not hard to tell that alcohol had been involved in this dinner party. Everyone, except my favorite Lt. Commander, of course, was laughing and hooting and hollering and generally raising hell. This was, of course, a very good omen for the up-coming operation we had hatched. As planned, Barney was going to talk with the General, who, as you may recall, was also getting flying lessons from Barney on the side. He put his arm out the window and motioned for the General to come over and talk to him and, sure enough, he did. You may not believe it but it is true. So part one of the plan was going into effect. We were covering our asses. Barney told the General the basics of our plan—that we were going to take the nurses to a party at our officers club at Ky Ha. Barney sure knew his "flight student" well since the General told him that it sounded like a good idea and he had no problems with it. Barney called me to say "It's okay with the General so we're good to go." Finally we were able to pry the paper-pushing staff types off our prizes and got the giggling bevy of girls onboard. Barney was, of course, free to go but guess who got to have the Lt. Commander in his jump seat? As you have probably guessed, he was completely pissed off.

They are late, the girls are uproariously drunk, and there was nothing of benefit in all of this for him. He started right in on me about hurrying up and getting back to the *Repose* ASAP. So it was up to me to explain to him that we really wanted to do that, but we now had a low fuel state and would be forced to go back to our base and refuel. Oh, that set him off but what the hell could he do about it? So Barney calls Ky Ha approach and asks for clearance for us both to land to the west. We were cleared and then did one of our lift offs and wide left hand turns in tight formation and came over the runway. We then taxied to the location on the flight line that we had all set up as a part of the plan. We shut down and with great ceremony explained to the nurses, and most especially to the Lt. Commander, that we would make special arrangements to get the refueling process expedited and it should be done in less than two hours. (It could have been done in ten minutes if we really had needed to go.) We also explained that they couldn't stay on the flight line. I then made the prearranged signal, and in drove an ambulance with our flight surgeon in command. We helped our guests as they all squeezed onto the bench seats along each side as well as onto the floor. I escorted the Lt. Commander to the passenger seat up front as if it was the place of honor, but really it was to get him the hell away from the nurses in the back. Barney and I hopped onto the back bumper and we started off the flight line and up the hill to the officers club. Barney and I could hardly believe we were pulling this off and were laughing like nut cases.

As Barney was helping our guests off the ambulance, I went into the club, which was pretty much in full swing by that time of night. I yelled out in my loudest voice, "Attention on deck!" Amazingly enough this actually brought silence as everybody stopped to figure out what the hell Boden was up to now, or had some high-ranking muckety-muck actually found his way to our hole-in-the-wall club? I immediately took full advantage of the silence and announced, "All present are hereby instructed to watch their language and conduct themselves as gentlemen because women are coming aboard." As you can imagine, this did nothing but cause a huge outflow of very loud and vile language mostly directed at my intelligence and family ancestry. However, I got the last laugh because, just at the height of this uproar, in walked the nurses. What a glorious moment that was! A complete, stunned silence filled the club. The nurses, having been so effectively pre-lubricated by our paper-pusher friends, got right into the mood and waded in, giving everybody the old "Hi, boys, haven't you seen a woman before?" and other assorted pokes and jabs.

There is no need to describe the drinking, yelling, and misguided moves our fellow pilots were trying to make, since it would be an embarrassment for all concerned. After about an hour of this, Barney and I knew we needed to get out of Dodge before something blew up this operation. We, of course, weren't able to drink, so the level of General stupidity being exhibited by all hands was getting pretty hard for us to swallow. I got up on the bar and announced that the birds were now refueled and ready to return to the *Repose*. We didn't need to take any other action as now the Lt. Commander, who had been such a pain in the side of progress, was now our ally as he took complete charge of rounding up his chicks and getting them loaded into the ambulance for the return ride to the flight line. With our "loaded" passengers now loaded back into the ambulance, we got back to the flight line. Then we got them onto the birds and back to the *Repose*, safe and unharmed, but with one hell of a good story to tell. Barney and I never heard a peep of reprimand, nor did we boast much, because when you get something right the first time, it's best to leave it alone.

All went very smoothly and Barney and I were the acknowledged heroes by the nurses and also by all of MAG 36. For the next few days the story was told and retold and grew more and more spectacular, just as if it was Dr. Seuss telling what he had seen on "Mulberry Street." I have no idea what happened on the *Repose* or the stories that they told, but I would dearly love to hear the nurses' side. Maybe one day one of the nurses that we flew will read this and contact me.

MAG 36 Officer's Club

USS Repose

After ten and one-half years with the Reserve Fleet at Suisan Bay, California, USS REPOSE was once again called to active duty. She returned to commissioned service in the U. S. Navy at 1400 on October 16, 1965 and within 151 days after call-up the USS REPOSE departed San Francisco on January 3, 1966. After refresher training and upkeep in Pearl Harbor, Hawaii and Subic Bay, Philippines, she arrived in Chu Lai, Republic of Vietnam on February 14, 1966. Vietnam marked the innovation of the concept of mobile hospital support. In this war, USS REPOSE was stationed offshore near the sites of the heaviest battles and took virtually all casualties aboard by helo. She was usually underway and seldom departed the combat zone. Her mission was her area of responsibility in I Corps Tactical Zone from Danang north to the DMZ (17th parallel). On January 30, 1967, she performed the 3000 consecutive successful helicopter landing. On March 29, 1967, she marked the 2000th surgical operation in Viet Nam.

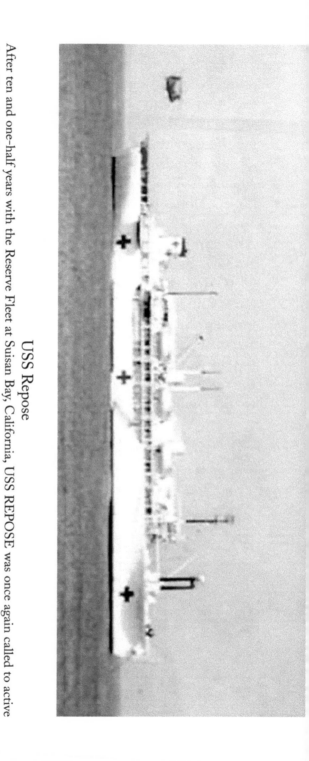

New Year's Eve Present

Ew Year's Eve was a cold and stormy night. There were no gala events to attend or any desire to even think about anything but staying warm and dry. I and most of the others stayed in our hooches and made dinner of C-rations to avoid having to go out in the rain to the mess hall. We then read, wrote letters, etc., and went to bed early.

The next morning, when I looked down at the flight line, I was surprised to see what looked like a flag pole with the American flag flying just past the seaward end of our runway. I got dressed and went down to learn that, not only was there a flag pole off the end of our runway, it was attached to a US Navy ship that was hard on the rocks and definitely not in a place that it had intended to be.

It turned out that the captain and crew of this fine vessel had felt that, since they were securely anchored and it was New Year's Eve, it would be okay to relax the regulations regarding drinking just a little, just for this one night. So someone had managed to find a source of booze which, of course, would never exist aboard except perhaps in the medicine locker. Wherever it was stored, it had found its way to the celebration and was evidently of sufficient quantity to bring a joyous and relaxed state to all hands.

With these few errors in judgment all coming together in the wee hours of January 1, 1967, fate took the next step and the anchor began to drag. But, of course, there was no one aboard who was sufficiently aware of his surroundings to realize it, until after a short while and there was a huge grinding crash followed by a few more lurches as the high seas pushed them foot by foot further up onto the rocks at the east end of our south runway.

They managed to do this at the peak of high tide so that no matter how hard they tried they were not going to get off. That fact, of course, did not stop them from trying. They had a lot of cement bags aboard so they began to unload them overboard, thinking that if the ship were lighter they could float off. It appeared, however, that the only thing that did was to effectively cement them to the rocks. They got a tug and pulled but to no avail. It was easy to imagine the morale aboard that ship, especially that of the captain who was surely going to be hung by his thumbs at his court-martial.

Someone did suggest that there was one advantage to the situation: the flag was an accurate and easily visible wind velocity and direction detector. We could even keep it in view as we were banking in our turns to keep from hitting it. Wind indicator be damned, we, of course, only wanted one thing to happen and happen right away and that was to get the damn mast with the flag flying from it cut off so we didn't have to dodge around it every time we took off. It took about three days for the Navy to give up, drop the flag, and cut the mast. It was a few more days before we stopped laughing as we realized how happy we were that it hadn't happened to one of us.

Bad End to New Years Eve Party

Going Down in the Valley

I guess I would have to classify this as a war story. I have told it a few times, and it is described in my Distinguished Flying Cross (DFC) citation written up by the H-46 leader. It's a mission I remember well and remain proud of, not because of some act of bravery but because of the number of unique solutions I needed to come up with to get out of the ever increasing mess into which the whole operation sank.

I was on assignment to support our sister squadron VMO-2 in Da Nang with my bird and the crew. It was three days after Christmas and we had been there for two days. I had already had some run-ins with some of the more "senior" though less experienced pilots. They thought that their rank was more important than the "Playboy" designation I had earned, and they wanted to be in charge of the flight. I needed to pull some BS like, "If you want me to help you out, you will do it my way or I am out of here." It rattled some cages but I had been there and done that before. There were plenty of assignments that needed to be filled where I could go if I showed up back at VMO-6, saying, "They didn't need me that bad." It may sound as if the strict ranking system the Marine Corps adheres to wasn't working, but when it comes to getting the job done, Marines always find a way.

It was a routine recon insertion, although it was a larger than normal team of about twenty-five to thirty men. I was leading, after another "take it or leave it routine" with a newbie Major who ended up as the pilot on my wing. Two H-46s would be the transports and we were to meet them right after takeoff from Marble Mountain. As was usual, the insertion was timed for just before dark to maximize the team's ability to escape detection or be followed by the Viet Cong. The landing zone (LZ) was just on the west side of a mountain ridge in a valley complex with a small river running through it. The surrounding ridge lines were at about 2,500 feet with the valley floor maybe 1,000 to 1,500 feet below. We had about a 3,000 foot ceiling so we could sneak under the clouds when crossing the ridge to let down into the LZ.

All went like clockwork. The LZ was easy to see and had plenty of room. I made a pass and all looked good so I cleared the 46s to land. In they went; their doors dropped and the team came running out, making for the cover of the tree line. They were keeping good separation from each other and the last of the team was just into the wood line and the birds were preparing to lift off when the radio came alive with the team leader shouting that they were under fire and had a man who was shot in the head. They needed covering fire and to get their wounded man out. The 46 leader came right up on the radio and told them they should stay put and wait. A ballsy decision, knowing they would be up to their ears in it very quickly and a big and easy target for the VC, who we now knew were right there and engaging the team.

I got the team leader to mark his position and was able to determine the location of the rest of the team, which was spread out in a line. He gave me the relative bearing to the enemy position, and my wingman and I set up covering fire for their move back to the LZ. We started by concentrating the fire to best help the part of the team nearest the LZ move back toward the 46s and set up a protective defense for the birds and their teammates as they moved out of the protective trees into the open LZ. When that was done, we changed to best cover the first part of the team, who were engaging the enemy and had the wounded man with them.

We kept up our covering fire; the 46s waited; five minutes went by, then ten minutes. I called the team leader to ask what was happening. They had more wounded and were coming as fast as they could. Well, fast wasn't the right word. It went on and on and it was now obvious that the whole team needed to be extracted, not just the wounded. The ceiling was lowering and it was getting darker by the minute. This was turning into a real can of worms and fast. Both I and the 46 leader were imploring the team to move faster. It was coming to the point where we were going to have to take the team members who had made it into the zone and leave, or all of us were going to be in the zone and under attack for the night, ill prepared and with no way to get any help. My wingman and I were near bingo fuel (the amount of fuel needed to get back to base); the ceiling was now below the ridge line, and gray was turning into black. I needed to find a solution better than leaving Marines in peril because very soon the only available course of action would be for me to order us to leave so we could save sixteen helicopter crewmen, the approximately ten team members already in the zone, and four helicopters. Leaving the balance of the team to fend for themselves overnight is the horrific type of decision that separates the men from the boys and was a Playboy's worst nightmare.

Both my wingman and I were now out of ammunition so our effectiveness was minimal. I remembered that our TACAN had a rarely used feature that allowed one aircraft to find the bearing to another by having one switch to a channel (I can't remember what the spread had to be) different than the one being used. So, while we still had some light left, I had my wingman switch to the appropriate TACAN channel and then follow the river to find the pass that had to exist somewhere when it exited the valley. As he left, I knew that at least one bird and its crew were moving out of harm's way.

To provide some kind of cover for the team, I continued to make what looked like strafing runs even though all we could do was throw any spent brass the crew could find lying around out the door as we went over the enemy position. We hoped that hearing it fall through the leaves would the VC think we were still shooting. The team was now making progress and the second 46 was now loaded and was able to lift off and start down the river while using his TACAN to track on my wingman. Soon after, the lead 46 had the last man on board; he lifted off and we both headed out with him tucked tight on my tail.

My wingman had found the pass and was circling, waiting for us. We soon arrived and were some happy campers to have escaped with everybody with us. But the two UH-1Es were still in big trouble. There was no way our fuel was going to get us back to Marble Mountain or any other place where we could land and be secure. Our only hope was an artillery outpost called An Ha. I called DASC (Direct Air Support Center) to get An Ha's radio frequency so we could make contact with them. I made the call and explained our predicament. We were about ten minutes away and they said, "You get here; we'll make a space for you both to land." The lead 46 stayed with us while the second, with wounded on board, had headed back to the hospital at Da Nang as soon as they had gotten out of the pass.

As you can tell, because I am writing the story, it all worked out. The artillery base got some lights to mark where we were to land, and we settled onto those skids with the biggest sigh of relief you have ever heard from a crew. The 46 left with the promise that he would be back at first light with fuel barrels and a pump. We met our new and very willing but concerned hosts. They were busy getting extra perimeter guards set up and a patrol organized, since they knew that they had just acquired a hugely attractive target for the VC to attack. So we may have felt a lot safer than we were a few minutes ago, but they now had a huge spike in their danger level.

We got some C-rations that we always kept on hand from our birds, ate, and were soon asleep in their command bunker. True to his word, there was the 46 at first light with our fuel. Our crews needed no encouragement to get it into the tanks, and we were soon able to thank our hosts and get back to Marble Mountain.

P.S. There was no more whining from my wingman, the newbie Major.

A Marine's Reflection on Being a Warrior

With some inspiration from a comment by Harry Hopkins about Roosevelt.

What a joy it is to find a time in your life when you can abandon thoughts of your own well-being, self interest and personal destiny as you immerse yourself in unimaginable, immeasurable risk for the benefit of others.

Out of Country

As you have surely realized by now, when it comes to working a good deal that turns into a lot of fun, I can rightfully be considered a master of the game. When it came to opportunities to get out of country I do not know of anyone that worked the system as well as I did, that is except Tony Pecoraro, who managed to get sent to Manila as the R&R (Rest and Relaxation) officer. He had great living quarters and was even able to have his wife join him for the two-plus months he was there.

I wasn't around the squadron a lot because I was often on detachment so if I was actually out of country, most never noticed. I managed to get out five times, and Laos, Thailand, and North Viet Nam don't count. It was routine to get one R&R per tour. It was not unusual in VMO-6 to get two R&Rs. A slick operator like me managed three—one to Hawaii and two to Hong Kong. Plus I managed orders to sea survival school in Japan with stops in Taiwan and Okinawa to get there. The routing caused such a big delay; well documented you can be sure, that I was "forced" to spend a week in Tokyo before reporting for the start of the next class. I felt so bad. I also went to Subic Bay in the Philippines on an emergency re-supply mission for liquor. So that is five times.

The first R&R, you may remember, came right after "The Longest Day." I opted for Hawaii so I could meet

162

my wife there. Ten days before leaving I had gotten all the arrangements made and my wife had all the information. Four days before I was to leave, I got a letter from her saying how excited she was to see me. She would be arriving the day before me, on November 21st. The 21st—holy crap—that was the week after I would be there! That night at midnight I got clearance to use the HAM radio set-up to patch a call to my father. He was pretty surprised to hear from me since it took an emergency situation to be able to make a call. I explained the problem; he told me he would do whatever needed to be done and get her there on time.

I walked off the plane and there she was, looking very good, I may add. It was a Sunday morning and, as I walked over, she took one look and said, "I'm going to church, and, if you want a kiss when I come back, you'd better have had a shower and shaved that stupid thing off your lip." I have always had a beard that grew like that of a fourteen year old with blonde hair. I had had the mustache about 2 to 3 months. The only reason you would even know it was there was because one side was dyed a nice reddish brown. Just the one side, since that was where I put the cigarettes I smoked copiously. It didn't take any time to decide to shave it off. As soon as I got to the hotel I was in the shower and became squeaky clean, closely shaved, and very kissable by the time church was over.

It was a wonderful time in Honolulu forty five years ago, with only a couple of hotels on the beach, plenty of great things to see and do, and no crowds. In what seemed like a day the week was over and I was back at war full speed ahead. What a mind warp.

It was mid-December, and I guess the CO realized I had been cranking out the missions and offered me an R&R to Hong Kong. Without a moment's hesitation and with a trip to the paymaster to get US dollars, I was off to Da Nang and aboard a Pan Am flight to Hong Kong. During the day I almost went broke saving money. A camera, a hi-fi setup, suits, clothes for my wife, shoes and more, all collected, crated and stored. At the end of the week it was tied into two loads for each side of the coolie's yoke. He stood up with the load on his shoulders and went running to the ferry with me chasing behind him, thinking this was going to be the last I ever saw of my stuff. It worked out okay. He led me directly to the shipping office, and I got it all labeled, addressed, and on its way home. Not the camera, of course. During the evenings I partied hard with a bunch of Aussies. The only thing I learned from them is that, if you think you can drink as much as they can, you will be wrong. Again, before I knew it, I was back in Viet Nam.

Next it was off to sea survival school. I believe it was an Air Force operation. My travel orders read to Tokyo by earliest available air and routing, then via train to the school, which was about 100 miles to the west of Tokyo. I was to report in at the school before the following Sunday. I arrived at CCK (Ching Chuan Kang Air Base) in Taiwan, where I was able to spend two nights and a day touring the city of Taichung, since there were no flights to Okinawa. The first afternoon was a Sunday and families were filling the parks with their children. Almost no one spoke English, but all were very friendly. I was able to unwind as I watched the peaceful, relaxed families just being themselves, laughing and smiling, playing with their children, and rowing boats in the lake. The next day, as I wandered around, I realized there were almost no cars; the sewer ran in the gutters; ox-drawn carts and coolies with back-breaking loads filled the streets, and life was very tough for everyone. I was back in Taiwan for business twenty years later and there was nothing but modern cities, cars, hotels and people in business dress everywhere. When Asians go to work, it is nothing short of miraculous to see what they can accomplish. If you have any thoughts that they will not catch up and pass us in economic power, you are wrong.

I was then on to Okinawa. The delay in Taiwan had given me an idea. If I was delayed a little bit more there in Okinawa, I wouldn't get to Tokyo in time to report to the school before Sunday. I explained the situation to the operations clerk who handled the travel orders and asked him if there was anything he needed me to pick up for him while I was touring the island for the next few days. I was not surprised to learn that a nice bottle of liquor would fit the bill, and he was sure that the first flight to Tokyo that I could get aboard would not be until Monday morning. He would be on duty Monday and would make sure everything was taken care of.

The best part of this trip was hiring a guide with a car who took me all over the place and explained the history and the World War II battles. I spent two days with him. I ate well, had steam baths and massages, and was very relaxed when I reported in on Monday morning for my flight. The gift was delivered and appreciated.

Tokyo was almost overwhelming. It made New York look like it wasn't crowded. I called the school to explain my absence and asked if it was okay to show up the next Saturday for that week's class. No problem was the answer, so I had six days to explore Tokyo. Almost no one spoke English so I had the hotel people write about a dozen phrases for me in both English and Japanese. Restaurant, taxi cab, bathroom, etc., and I was off. One evening I got a taxi and wanted to go to what I was trying to describe as a local family-type restaurant. As you may guess, it wasn't working and the driver kept thinking that, like most stupid Americans, I wanted go to the Ginza district with all the glitz and night clubs. Finally at one point when we were in a normal looking area, I just got out and started walking. It wasn't long, after sticking my head into different businesses, that I found what looked like the perfect place. They were not very busy and were pretty surprised to see this "giant" American show up at their door. With much bowing and ceremony to get me seated they gave me a menu. That didn't help much but suddenly you could see the mama-san who was in charge light up with an idea. She took me by the arm and we went outside and around the corner of the building where, lo and behold, they had a display case with plastic models of the food they served. Perfect. I pointed out five or six different items and we went back inside, where she started giving orders, and the meal began. I got a beer and could tell they were really getting into the idea of feeding this stranger. There was no language but we were getting a good communication going. I was there for about an hour and a half and was having a great time. Other customers arrived; no one could speak English, but they were getting into the scene. When I was finally done and in the process of paying the bill, in came a young man with his golf clubs, who obviously was just returning from having played. The family was glad to see him. He had me sit back down as they all started to tell him excitedly about what had been going on. He was mama-san's son and spoke English. It was like a bursting dam since they were finally able to talk with me through him. Not only was I able now to effectively thank them for doing so well in meeting and exceeding my expectations for the restaurant I had pictured, but also for the wonderful food. He told me I was a big hit with his family and they, too, had had a wonderful time, and there was enough thank-you and bowing going on that it took five minutes for me to back out into the street and leave. I just love Asians and somehow seem to find it very easy to connect with them even without language. I think in a past life I was a navigator aboard the earliest ships that came from Europe to begin trade with Asia in the fifteen hundreds. That's my story and I will stick with it; you can believe it or not.

On Saturday I boarded the bullet train to head for the school. This was the only high speed train in the world and it was something else. When we went into a tunnel, my ears would pop because of the rapid increase in the air pressure. I was very impressed. I arrived at about 4:00 on Saturday afternoon and checked in. There were only two of the dozen or so students that would make up the class, and the staff asked us to go with them for dinner and drinks on the town. What I remember most was when I was in the restaurant's bathroom, standing at the urinal doing my thing, a young woman came out of the stall and stood right next to me washing her hands and chatting coolly with me in Japanese. I was struck dumb and just stood there with not only my fly open but now my mouth as well. I came out right behind her with a startled look to see the staff all watching me and laughing their heads off. It was soon explained to me that the Japanese actually understand how both male and female bodies work in the process of eliminating the body's waste and see no reason to use up valuable space having separate facilities. Our western attitude is pretty silly when you think about it.

My next trip out was to Subic Bay in the Philippines. It had recently been learned that the staff sergeant who was in charge of running our officers club had managed to skim off 36,000 dollars during the time he was in charge. This led to a Major break down in the liquor supply and very soon there was no hard liquor to be had. As you must realize by this point in my tales, this was a desperate situation and called for desperate action. Arrangements were made for the squadron Executive Officer to borrow the old R-4 (same as a DC-3, twin engine cargo plane built in 1940s) that was kept next door at Chu Lai and go to the Philippines. I smelled a good deal right away and volunteered to take the orders and collect the money from the other thirsty members of the squadron. It was only one small step from this job to be seen as the most logical choice to go and help with the purchase, packing, and distribution of the quest. Aha, I did it again!

Off we went on a beautiful sunny morning for what was to be about six to seven hours to cover the thousand miles. It was a chance for me to go to sleep since I had none of the skills needed to fly this old lady. It turned out that I may not have been alone in the low skill category on this flight. We had been out about five or six hours when the starboard engine began to start running a little rough. It was easy to feel and I knew what a rough engine was. It wasn't bad but, as we proceeded, it began to get a little worse. Piston-driven aircraft engines have dual ignition systems so that, if one fails, the other will keep the engine operating, a very good plan indeed. Before every flight, just before being cleared onto the runway for takeoff, one of the standard procedures is to do a magneto check—run the engine up and then shut off one ignition system and then the other to assure that they are both operating properly. If one system is found not to be working, you never switch it back on, but let the engine stop so you don't blow up the motor with a huge backfire. Notice that the procedure is done on the ground. It is a cardinal rule that a magneto check is never to be done in flight. Well, of course, you now know where I am going with this. Sure enough, we were about 300 miles from Subic, over the open ocean, when our fearless leader decided to check out the situation by doing a magneto check. You guessed it; one system was down and the motor stopped, but not for long since the good magneto was switched immediately back on and with a very significant backfire. Thank God, it settled down and kept on running. Yes, rough, but running. Within a couple of hours my heart rate was back below 100 and we were setting up for our approach to the runway. I had my nose pressed against a port hole to see Subic Bay, the ships, and the countryside when, just as we were turning off the downwind leg, the window popped out and left me with my face literally hanging in the breeze. It scared me so bad I almost peed in my pants. We landed safely and I was damn glad to have my feet back on solid ground.

169

We quickly went to the club to get a drink and settle our jangled nerves. Years later, when we gave the base back to the Philippines, the Subic Bay Officers Club was dismantled and sent to the Naval Air Museum in Pensacola and reassembled. When I went to the club at the museum, it reminded me of the R-4 ride, and it took a lot of the joy away from eating my lunch.

Since the engine needed work, we were not going to be able to return the next morning as planned. Ah, gee, that's too bad. I, as usual, had some civilian clothes with me just in case such a problem arose. That night I went into Olongapo, the Asian equivalent of Tijuana. I went to two of the clubs, the East End Club and the West End Club. One was as raunchy as the other. The highlight of the night was when a group of us left the East End to go to the West End. We needed two of the jitney cabs to get us there. We, of course, immediately turned it into a race with ten dollars to the winning driver to be paid by the losing passengers. We quickly realized that this may not have been the smartest thing we ever did since the drivers took on the challenge and went into "win or die trying" mode. Off we went, up on the sidewalks, down the wrong side of the street, cutting each other off, until we came to a screeching halt in front of the West End Club. I do not remember who won and none of us cared; we were so glad to have survived the ride without bodily injury. The next day we got the liquor purchased; the plane was ready to go so we loaded up and made an uneventful return flight the next morning.

My last R&R was another "right time right place" happening with unbelievable odds. I was going back to Hong Kong for a second time. I got on a hop to Da Nang to get the flight to Hong Kong that was to leave at about noon. There was a delay because, would you believe it, a magneto on one of the four engines needed to be replaced. I was beginning to wonder about me and magnetos. To fill the time I went to the Air Force club. What a fancy joint—air conditioning, carpet—you wouldn't even know you were in Viet Nam. The party was soon under way, and the group, which was a mix of services and duties, got into the spirit of going on vacation and were well lubricated after four hours had gone by and we finally boarded to take off.

I immediately fell asleep and didn't wake up until we were about forty-five minutes out of Hong Kong. I started chatting with the Corporal in the seat next to me and pretty soon he said to me, "See that stewardess (this was in the days when they were stewardesses, not flight attendants), the good looking one?" "Yes," I responded. "She was right here staring at you two or three times while you were sleeping," he said. I looked up at her and she came walking over and asked, "Do you know who I am?" "I am sorry, no." I answered She then said, "You're John Boden from Middle Haddam, Connecticut." I was dumb-founded as she went on to say "I am Vicky Beilman and we went to grammar school together." Unbelievable, she was my first love, who sat across from me in the fifth and sixth grades. She was the first girl I ever "dated," when a group of us went horseback riding. I had even been able to save her when her horse took off galloping back to the barn. Kismet was in full bloom this day. We made arrangements to meet that night at a party with a bunch of the Pan Am pilots and crew. Her friends and

171

I toured all the attractions during the day and partied at night. It was a damn good week since this little part of my life walked in and then back out, like a dream. If you saw it in a movie, you wouldn't have believed it.

Haiwii Sunset Crusie

Okinawa Tombs Shaped Like Wombs

Taiwan Dried Fish for the Really Hungry

Japan Sea Survival School

East End Club

Vicky and Friend At Walled City, Hong Kong

More information and photos at
www.klondikeplayboy.com

SOG Operations

I spent many days and weeks flying for the SOG (Studies and Observation Group) of MACV (Military Assistance Command Viet Nam). This was to support ultra-secret, black operations going into Laos and Cambodia in order to monitor and interdict the movement of men and supplies down the Ho Chi Minh Trail. There were six ARVN Air Force H-34s, call sign, King Bee, operating as transports, and we were usually two birds acting as their gun cover and as TACA for them and the fixed wing air strikes. The H-34s were old and in rugged shape. The leader had both VHF and FM radios; the rest had either one or the other, and many times the birds in the middle of their in-line formation had neither working. A couple of the birds were so old they had the exhausts coming out the lower left of the cowling. Sikorsky had made a modification almost immediately to move the exhaust to the upper left because it was starting fires whenever they landed in grass or brush. The crews were being paid $500 for each trip over the border and managed to get that worked out so it was $500 in and $500 out. Thus they had a lot of incentive not to complain about details like radios. Their leader was known as Cowboy, and he was widely known and hugely respected for the hundreds of times he pulled off incredible feats that saved a lot of people. Frankly, they earned the money. It was we Marines who were being under-paid.

Normally, with a couple of memorable exceptions, we did not get a lot of fire from the ground on these missions because, when the insertions and extractions were done, we tried to pick LZs that would not be seen by the enemy, even though it meant a lot of travel on foot to the team's actual destination. It was both safer and more effective. Often times Marine Recon insertions inside Viet Nam involved our putting the teams in pretty close to the enemy positions and way too often taking them out when the enemy was all over them, giving rise to a lot more risk and danger.

The air strikes were usually run on targets that were identified with coordinates where the inserted teams had found supplies, and then we only ran them when the team had gotten well away. One of the indicators that we had hit the right spot was secondary explosions. There could not be a better or more satisfying confirmation. The biggest cache that they discovered had tons and tons of munitions and other supplies, including rice. It was like the 4th of July grand finale, the big daddy of the secondary explosions. We referred to the spot as the rice pile and, whenever any of the jets had unexpended bombs or napalm, we would have them drop them on the rice pile on their way home. They continued for days to get more explosions and burn more rice. It was easy to see—the only big brown and white (the rice) spot cut out of the green jungle. We would go out just before sunrise at treetop level and catch the enemy re-bagging rice. There had to be tons of it. No matter what we did, there was always more rice left.

The teams were made up of Nungs or Montagnard tribesmen with two or three US Army Special Forces who were the SOG leaders and sometimes a dog. The French term "Montagnard" means "from the mountains" and refers to the indigenous people from the Central Highlands of Viet Nam, made up of multiple tribal groups. The Nung were a Chinese ethnic group recruited mainly from the Saigon area. They would tap North Vietnamese Army (NVA) telephone lines or plant acoustic and seismic sensors along the Ho Chi Minh Trail. I remember listening one time when a Nung translator was there and the NVA had found one of the devices which had been hidden in a tree. We could hear a lot of jabbering and the sounds of somebody climbing up the tree to get it. It was then dropped onto the ground and caused even louder yelling as they tried to figure out how to shut it off. When they couldn't, it suddenly stopped transmitting with a crunch. They must have stomped on it.

We operated out of a small airstrip at Kham Duc, which was almost due west of Chu Lai over the mountains. We stayed there overnight sometimes, but, since it was not very secure for the birds because they were parked on the airstrip that was outside of the defensive perimeter of the base compound, we more often went to a small SOG outpost just south of the city of Kon Tum, along with the ARVN H-34s. We all landed right inside the secure compound, where they had a barracks for us and, even more importantly, a club and a bar.

The Montagnards were the defensive unit that protected the Kham Duc perimeter. They were from a local tribe and had their wives and children living right in the bunkers with them. There was never a reason to worry about their loyalty. Also, we could observe the daily routine of their lives. Each morning the women went down off our hilltop position to get water. They carried large bamboo tubes in baskets on their backs which they filled and carried back up to their homes. It was quite a load on their way back up the hill when they were full. They also had a big broom-making operation. They cut reeds at the river's edge and then spread them out in every available open space to dry. The next step was to tie the stalks together, making a handle about three feet long and two inches in diameter. This left the fuzzy bristles coming off the handle at a perfect angle for sweeping. I had seen these brooms all over Viet Nam and now knew how they were made. Women's Lib may have been starting in the States but surely not here in these indigenous tribes where the women did the work.

I also learned about another local practice, which was centered on the ohhhhhh jug. The reason it was named the "ohhhhhh jug" was "ohhhhhh" was the sound you made when you awoke in the morning and felt the pain in your head. It was a large jug of rice wine with some other unknown and surely disgusting ingredients added. I only tried this once and after my first drink quickly learned to pretend to drink when the jug came around again. I was able to be polite and accept their hospitality and what they considered the honor to have been invited to drink with them, yet not suffer what some described as a near death experience in the morning.

I have three stories to relate from my times with SOG. The first is about how the genius of my crew chief Sgt. Cullum and the connections of the SOG people kept us in the air. When it came to connections, the SOG people

179

had them. What SOG wanted, SOG got. One morning at Kham Duc, when I went to start the bird, it was dead. Sgt. Collum determined that the starter generator was down. There were no magic tricks for that. Only a new part was going to fix it. There were missions to fly that day; therefore the other bird was going to be unable to make a parts run and would be doing the missions alone. So Sgt. Collum came up with an idea. They took the starter generators off both birds, put the good one on my bird and we started it. Then they took it back off while the engine was running, and put the bad one back on. We quickly determined that the generator function was fine. They put the good one back on the other bird and got it started. While we were doing this, the SOG boys were on the radio and had made arrangements for us to go to Pleiku, a huge Army Air Base, and have a new starter generator installed. They gave me the Army unit's name to ask for when I contacted the tower for landing and a bottle of scotch for the sergeant I was to deal with at the unit. Don't ask me where they came up with a bottle of scotch out there in that forsaken place. They told me to give him the scotch, and he would take care of everything I needed.

We took off and headed south past Kon Tum to Pleiku. I couldn't believe it when I saw it. It was huge and with more helicopters on it than I think the whole Marine Corps owned. Our base at Ky Ha could have fit inside any one individual unit's area. The difference in how much it cost the government to run the Marine Corps versus the Army was strikingly obvious when I looked at this operation.

We were soon at our destination, had met our contact, delivered the goods, and were getting service as if we were the long lost country cousins from the farm. They couldn't have been nicer and were in complete awe of our bird. They had never seen a UH-1E model configuration before. Things like the hoist and the rotor brake looked very cool to them. But what impressed them the most was its General condition. They had never seen bullet holes and cracks in the Plexiglas that were drilled and then knitted together with wire to keep the breaks from growing. They had never realized how well beer cans worked to patch holes in the skin, or that skids which had had a few hard landings (not mine) were okay because the body of the bird was still not touching the ground, even though by only a few inches. There were many details that caused a steady parade of sightseers coming to see what the Marine Corps was "forced" to work with. I think the biggest curiosity was our gun sight system. We used a spot on the windshield and a fold-down rod attached above the windshield with an open circle on the end. In the circle were two wires, one vertical, and one horizontal, making the crosshairs. Line up the crosshairs and the spot on the windshield by pointing the plane at the target and let the guns and/or rockets go. Worked great for us, but they couldn't believe it.

When we left the next day, wined and dined, our bird was not the same as she had been when we had brought her there. I don't remember the whole list, but new rotor blades, all new Plexiglas, new skids, a reflex gun sight, wash and shine inside and out, and, of course, a new starter generator. We left to go back to work with thanks to our new friends. It was a couple of weeks before I got back to the squadron. I was quite proud of the fix we had pulled off and all the neat new parts we had acquired. When KD heard about it, I thought he was going to have a nervous break down. "How the hell am I going do the paperwork for the parts you lost and these new ones with part numbers that don't even exist in the Marine Corps?" he ranted. Of course he found out a way and I learned much, much later from Dave Ballentine that he actually figured out how to get back to Pleiku and dip into the parts source I had discovered. Love the Army when you need more gear!

The next story doesn't have a bad ending, but it damn near did. A new wingman showed up one day to rotate with the other crew and bird. The pilot was a new captain whom I had met once or twice but had not flown with or heard much about. He was pretty excited about the idea of going on secret missions into Laos and seemed ready to get into action as soon as possible. We had a routine insertion that afternoon so we suited up and took off after getting briefed. As usual it called for sneaking them in and then getting out of there and back home, doing our best not to be seen. I found and checked out the LZ, got Cowboy and his King Bees set up, and they inserted the team. They took off and we started home. My wingman called to say he had spotted a hut at the edge of a clearing and was going down to check it out. This was not part of "get in and get out as fast and unobtrusively as possible," so I told him to forget it and join up. Captain Gung Ho paid no attention and down he went. "It will only take a minute," was his response to my telling him to get back on my wing so we could get the hell out of there.

Not only did he not get back in formation, but he actually landed in the clearing and had one of his crew jump out and run over to the shack to see if he could see anybody. He was trying to stir up trouble. He got trouble but not the kind he was anticipating. It was hot as hell that day and he had landed at about 2,000 feet above mean sea level. Guess what, he didn't have the power to lift off. I was out of my tree at this point when I realized what his problem was. He was somewhat humbler now so was at least listening to me. "Jettison your rocket pods." He still couldn't lift, "Dump your 7.62 ammo." He still couldn't lift. His crew chief got under the bird and started draining fuel and after about fifteen very tense minutes he got it off the ground, and we went back to Kham Duc. I told him to stay with his bird while the crew refueled and I went up the hill to debrief. Cowboy had already delivered the news about this jerk's escapade, so all I had to do was ask the SOG people to wave their magic wand and get another crew in there. This guy is done! In ten minutes it was set. I would handle the missions in the morning myself and the replacement would be there in the afternoon. I went back to the field and told Captain Gung Ho to take off and get directly back to Ky Ha as fast as possible; they could deal with him there. I wish I could tell you that every Klondike pilot was great, but I can't. I hoped it would be FAC (forward air controller) duty for him, which is what, happened, for a while anyway. He would be on the ground living with grunts so that his only contact with an aircraft would be by radio.

The next story is grab ass-based so I am sure you won't be surprised to learn that it started in a bar. We were all back at the outpost south of Kontum and would be there for the weekend. We had a great time at the club on Friday night with our good friends the Army Special Forces gang running the SOG missions. As you can well imagine, they were very, very tough and dedicated soldiers. They never hesitated to hang their asses as far out as was needed to get the job done. They were as loyal to the Nungs and the Montagnard tribesmen that they employed as they would have been to their own little brothers. Gaining these men's respect and knowing that they often requested me to be their support made me proud. Being respected for the job I did, by men I respected, for the job they did, was the juice that kept me going.

With this kind of respectful relationship, filled with testosterone and then mixed with liberal quantities of alcohol, you have to know that there would be a lot of bragging and challenges about who had the biggest set of *cojones*. As this banter progressed and moved from one topic to the next, it was pretty tough for a pilot-type to stay ahead of guys like these. At one point the challenge was, "If you have never jumped out of an aircraft, you can't even pretend to be a real man." Being of quick wit and pickled brain, I quickly answered, "Get parachutes and a plane, and we'll jump anytime, anywhere." This caused a moment of silence from one end of the club to the other, all twenty to thirty feet of it. "You're on. Tomorrow morning at nine," the SOG leader yelled, throwing down the gauntlet.

Uh, oh, I did it again. I looked around at the other seven Marines, who, without a bit of hesitation, nodded to me their assent to take the challenge for all of us. So it was agreed; we were all doing our first parachute jump in the morning. At that point in the evening we all thought this was a hell of a good idea, so we had a couple more drinks and went to bed.

In the light of day the next morning, there were eight Marines trying to pretend there hadn't been any challenges and acceptances the night before, but we were quick to realize as we headed to breakfast that all that gear and those guys getting things ready over by the parachute jump training area hadn't forgotten, and the challenge was still on.

We began our extensive jump training. The Army does all parachute training for all services, so this would not be different, except in a couple of minor ways. Regular training lasts three weeks; ours lasted thirty minutes. Two jumps off the platform to learn the land-tuck-and-roll maneuver, which seven of the eight actually learned pretty well. More on that later. That was exception number one. The second exception was that we would be jumping in full sport chutes meant only for use by experienced and seasoned jumpers. They had two panels removed to allow them to be steered and directed for more control by the jumper and also to facilitate a faster rate of descent. We were shown where the toggle handles were stowed in little bags on the riser harness and instructed that pulling down on the right one rotated you to the right and vice-versa. Maybe one or two of us got this lesson, but I was not one of them so you will hear more on that later, also.

With our training complete we piled onto a truck with parachutes, helmets, etc., and headed out of the compound to rendezvous with one of the King Bee H-34s at a big open field north of the outpost just across the highway from Kon Tum. We arrived just as King Bee landed to find that, security be damned, the word was out and there were hundreds of locals, more than half of them kids, there for the pending excitement. There were even a couple of pedal-type bicycle ice cream carts trying to make a buck at the grand event. There was excitement in the air and the kids were everywhere around us. The SOG people helped get us all suited up and checked and rechecked that all was right with the gear. The kids would have gotten into the bird with us if there had not been some stern discipline finally brought to bear.

Off we went, climbing to 3,000 feet. We circled a few times while the jumpmaster dropped a couple of wind dummies. Wind dummies were not one of us Marines but a small chute that he could watch to determine how the wind would affect us during the descent. He did determine that the wind was up to about fifteen knots, which we learned later was at or over the limit for us to jump. He told us to keep facing to the north when we were going down and asked if we wanted to chicken out. You know our answer to that, so he had us stand, line up and hook our static lines onto a cable they had rigged near the door. He directed Cowboy to the position over the ground he wanted and yelled, "Go!" as he whacked each of us on the ass on the way out the door. We went in pairs on each pass over the zone with never a second of hesitation, a fact that was toasted by the jumpmaster that night at the bar.

I have one overwhelming memory and that is that, when the chute opened, I felt like I was suspended motionless with the most incredible view of the world you could imagine. I hung there agog and awed for what seemed like ten minutes (probably thirty seconds) until I glanced down and realized that the ground was coming screaming up at me. "Holy crap, get it together!" I began to size up the situation and soon realized I was facing south, not north, and was headed beyond the field into the trees. Not having learned my lesson as well as I should have about the control line toggles, I hunted franticly to find them. Nope, they were not there. Of course they were there, but on the outside of the harness risers, where I couldn't see them, an important part of the lesson I hadn't learned. So I started pulling on one of the harness risers to get turned to the north facing into the wind. It worked, although I learned afterward that doing that is a no-no and quite dangerous. I was turning to the north, which was slowing my movement over the ground, which had been the fifteen miles per hour of wind speed plus the twelve miles per hour of speed the chute moves away from the two empty panels that are spilling air, or twenty-seven knots total when I was going south. It was a big relief to see the speed over the ground reducing to near zero as I came to face the north, even though old Mother Earth was still coming up at a pretty good clip. Problem, problem. I didn't stop turning as I reached north but kept on turning. There was no more time for any more maneuvering as the earth and I were soon to become one. My eyes grew wider and wider as I watched my speed over the ground grow faster and faster. I was much relieved, however, to see that what was going to be a full 360° turn had at least reduced my southern travel enough that I would land in the field a few feet short of the trees. I hit, and I mean "hit," the ground. Land-tuck-and-roll, and I became a cloud of dirt and dust and pain. Twelve miles per hour vertically and twenty-seven miles per hour horizontally was pretty much like a car wreck without the car. Of course, nothing less would do than to leap up with a cheer, raising my arms to signal that all was well. A couple of the kids were there first, and they were a great help in gathering up the chute and helping me carry it back to the truck.

The only reason I can remember that I was one of the first to jump was that I got to watch and snap a few pictures of some of the others after I arrived back on the ground. Everyone did great and there were no injuries, except one. Remember land-tuck-and-roll. If you decided to use the pile driver style instead, it was a lot harder to get up when your body was compressed into a position that you had not been in since before you were born. Look at the photo of the pile driver technique and notice that the risers are still taut and holding the jumper's weight, a situation that ended just one micro-second after the picture was taken and resulted in the full effect of the crash coming upon the poor guy's unsuspecting body. Only a sprained ankle resulted, although we did not think to measure his height to see how much shorter he had become.

It was a grand time in the club that night with eight new members being accepted as "one of the boys" in a group where only a man was considered to be one of the boys. We had to send our wounded comrade back for replacement with strict orders that he tell only one story, the one about stepping in a hole and twisting his ankle. It was twenty-five years later at a reunion in Jacksonville, North Carolina, that the squadron skipper heard about the jump and was torn between being completely pissed off and laughing himself silly, even with all that time gone by.

You couldn't make up stuff like this; only real life could be this far off the wall.

SOG Leaders

Montanard Native Village

Making Brooms

Suiting Up To Jump

Kids At The Jump

Full Sport Chute
(notice empty steering panels)

Piledriver Landing
(notice the risers are still tight and the crash will happen
in one micro-second)

They Were There and Then They Weren't

I am including this story, not because there were heroics, historical significance, or a Major effect on a battle. I include it as an illustration to show how something that happened in an instant could cause such shock and awe that anyone who was there will never get it out of his mind. That even when you are doing everything exactly right, everything can still go completely wrong. And, but for the grace of God, that could have been me or my family mourning my death and knowing I would never be part of the family again.

It was the 5th of April, 1967. We were on a twenty-four hour medevac tour, and we were almost ready to be relieved. VMO-6 was doing both halves that day—flying a slick for the pickup as well as the gunship. More often we flew the gunship with an H-34 or H-46 flying the pickup. We had done a number of missions, and we had been switching pilots back and forth between flying the pickup and the gunship. I can't say exactly, but we had probably done six to eight missions during the last twenty-three hours. When the call came for this one, I was up for pilot of the gunship and Al Dean and Brooke Shadburne flew the slick. I do not remember who my co-pilot or crew was for this mission I thought Al was in the right seat of the slick for this flight, but the record shows that it was Brooke. They were both well-qualified, experienced pilots and good friends, so it could have been either way.

I got all the frequencies and plotted the TACAN position from the coordinates, ran out to my bird, and taxied for takeoff right behind Al and Brooke. We were headed for the Duc Phu area, where Operation Desoto was underway. It was about twenty-five miles south, near the border of I Corps and II Corps and about four to five miles west of the beach. The pickup was on a large, flat hilltop for two wounded Marines. We were directed to the northeast area of the hill, where the wounded had been brought to avoid the area to the south of the hill, from which the Marines were receiving sporadic fire from the enemy. Al and Brooke made a spiraling approach to the landing zone, where the wounded waited with the four men carrying them. As the bird flared into a hover in preparation for landing, the four Marines began to run towards it with the wounded on litters. Just before they set down from their hover, a huge explosion occurred and everyone and everything just seemed to disappear. Completely gone, a black mark left where men and machine had existed. It didn't seem possible, but it was true. The crew in my plane and I were stunned, shocked into silence. First we saw them and then we didn't.

We had work to do, stunned or not. I had to get back into action. I had a bird to fly and plans to make. I contacted the troops on the south of the hill, but they had no explanation of what had happened. We then made immediate contact with the DASC (Direct Air Support

Center) to request additional medevac pickup birds and another gunship to support us. They estimated about one hour before their arrival. We then made contact with the headquarters base for Operation Desoto, located on the west side and at the bottom of the hill. To conserve fuel I landed at their position. We were able to learn in detail the ground situation and maintain contact to be ready to assist and provide cover for the birds en route.

Darkness was fast approaching in the interim, but the planning we were able to do while at the HQ and the coordination with the troops on the ground, who had gathered what were now ten KIA instead of the two wounded marines, allowed us to be effective in directing the new arrivals. One was an H-46 for the pickup and the other was a squadron mate from VMO-6 in a gun bird. When they were about ten miles out, I launched to join up and began directing what was now a whole new operation. Since there were now ten KIA and, I also believe, an additional WIA instead of the original two WIA, even the H-46 was going to have a full bird. There had been no new contact with the enemy since the explosion, and the troops on the ground seemed to have everything under control. I knew there couldn't be any more explosives hidden where the first one went off so I decided the H-46 should go back into the same area for the pickup. It also meant that the troops on the ground didn't have to move the dead any further away from where they were gathered. My wingman joined up on me and we began runs on the north side of the pickup bird to be ready to lay down protective cover should they start to receive any enemy fire. All went as smooth as a baby's ass and the H-46 lifted off in less than five minutes with all the KIA and WIA on board. They then headed straight back to Chu Lai on their own.

Now the two of us had to get home. Not as easy as you may think since the ceiling had come down to under 500 feet and it was now as dark as the inside of your eye lids. It was apparent very soon that staying VFR (Visual Flight Rules) under the cloud cover was not going to work. The homebound H-46 reported that the cloud cover was just a little over 2,000 feet thick and that they were VFR on top. I told my wingman to separate and start a climb through the goop on a heading of 360° degrees until he broke out on top and I would meet him there. I started my climb on a heading of 090° so we would keep well away from each other until we came out on top. We would join up again when we were in the clear. I shut off my anti-collision light, standard procedure, to help prevent vertigo. The red rotating light, reflecting off the goop onto the instrument panel, with the added strobe effect of the rotor blades flashing past, made instrument flying next to impossible with it turned on. It was just about one minute later; all was fine and we were climbing at 500 feet per minute, still IFR (Instrument Flight Rules), when we saw an anti-collision rotator beacon cut right across in front of us in a steep descent, coming from our aft, left, and then disappear. "Holy Crap, Klondike Two, you damn near killed us," I yelled into the radio. "Pull up, pull up, and get on your gauges. You are descending and heading southeast." "Pulling up," he responded. "Get your co-pilot on the controls with you and shut off your anti-collision light," I shouted. This was the second time on this one flight that "I saw them and then I didn't". Also the second time I had had my heart shocked so badly it nearly stopped, to say nothing about how my underwear was holding up. I guess from the point of view of the crew in the other bird it was damn lucky for them that they almost killed us, or we would never have been able to warn them. You can figure out how the rest of that story would have ended.

We were soon both out of the cloud cover on top and joined back up. I contacted Chu Lai approach for a radar-vectored GCA (Ground Controlled Approach) to get us back through the goop to land at Ky Ha. They came back and said they had us on their radar, told us to stay on our present course, and reported their ceiling at 500 feet. "Roger. Staying on our northbound course. My wingman is having issues with vertigo so he will be descending with me in tight formation. Over." "Roger. You will both be making one approach together," they replied. When the TACAN was showing us about one mile due west of the airfield, Chu Lai approach called, "You are both cleared to turn to a heading of 090° and begin a descent at 500 feet per minute. When you can see the water, you are cleared VFR and can switch to Ky Ha tower for landing instructions. Over." "Roger. Cleared VFR when the water is sighted and switch to Ky Ha tower," I acknowledged. Only in Viet Nam would anyone ever get a GCA like that. "Klondike Two, you and your co-pilot get on the controls together and shut off your anti-collision light, and I will, also. When you are comfortable, let me know. Over," I called. The rotators went off and number two replied, "We are ready. I have your navigation lights. Lead the way." "Beginning the descent," I answered.

There were no more problems and we landed. It was the end of a very, very long and tough day. There were many tough flights, but none so emotionally devastating for me as this one. The loss of good friends in such a quick and unexplainable way and with such a close call with disaster for a second time on the same flight lingers with me to this day.

We learned later that it was a 500 lb. bomb with wires leading from it to VC waiting in hiding that caused this most unique and horrible incident.

There are quite a number of people who have contributed content about this incident on the Pop-A Smoke WEB site *www.popasmoke.com* under *Viet Nam, KIA Incidents, date 670406 = April 6th 1967.*

Coming Home

The end of this war was finally coming for me. The Army personnel spent a year in country. Marines also spent a year in country but we, of course, are tougher and meaner so our year lasted thirteen months. I guess the powers that be used a baker's dozen as their measure. I do not remember an attitude change as I entered "short timer" status and do not think I stopped flying until two to three days before leaving. I do remember that, as the end was coming, and with orders in hand, we all would announce our status each day: ten days and a wake-up, nine days and a wake-up, etc. There were no parties, no ceremonies, just a few quiet good-byes and we just slipped away and weren't there anymore. After the mass exodus of the original Klondikers, almost a year before, there were only eight or ten pilots who had finished a tour before me and gone home, and it was the same thing for them. What could you say anyway? The only exception I recall is when the Group CO was leaving. There was a big party in the club. It was pretty loud and the open bar had made a lot of drunks when the Lycoming Rep, a big buddy of the CO, started to call for attention so the CO could sprinkle his wisdom upon us with his final words. There was still no reduction in the General mayhem after three tries so the Rep whips out his 45 and shoots three times through the roof. It worked, we were very quiet. Shooting rounds on base was definitely not cool, but who was going to say anything to the CO's main sidekick?

The only event I recall of my ride back to the States was watching two sunrises while on one flight. We took off early and soon saw the sun rise and, as we raced to the east, the sun raced to the west and met us again before we got to the States. It was a very long ride, but no one complained since it was the ride we had all been waiting a long time to take.

In mid 1967 there was a lot of anti-war sentiment but not yet at the levels that would soon follow in the years ahead. We were briefed to keep cool and, if possible, to get into civilian clothes as soon as possible once we were in the real world. I did not have any incidents and quickly slid back into normal life as the warrior in me melted away.

Arriving at home was wonderful. Giving everyone a hug and feeling their relief that I was back well and safe, helped acclimate me very quickly. I recall only one incident that scared my wife. On the first or second night home I got up in the middle of the night, went to the window and peeked out. I started directing the movement of troops based on what I thought I was seeing. I awoke in the middle of this and turned to see my wife sitting up in the bed completely flabbergasted. That was the first and the last time any issues like this arose. We didn't know about PTSD (Post Traumatic Stress Disorder) at that time, and I never felt that I was affected by it in the way that caused so many to suffer so much. For myself and the others I knew who were in Viet Nam, there was no remembering, no retelling, no war stories; it was just over and done with. Everyone had a very personal experience and knew that no else had an experience like theirs. Some were proud, some were angry, some were ashamed, some were never in any real danger, some felt fear and it controlled them, some never felt fear, and many, like me, felt fear and carried on in spite of it. We did not want to be judged on our performance in our unique experience because no else could understand it; so surely we were not going to judge others whose unique experience we could never understand. This led to only one course of action: shut up, suck it up, and get over it, no matter what your "it" was.

My wife and I soon were organized and ready to move back to our old stomping grounds in New River, North Carolina, to complete my Marine Corps service. I had made a big splurge and bought my wife a brand new Triumph Spit Fire. We could order a foreign car while we were in Viet Nam and have it shipped to the US duty free. I was a big hit the day I showed up with it after picking it up in New York with the help of my brother. It did mean we would be driving two cars back to North Carolina. A call to our old landlord, Lloyd Respass, let us know that the house we had rented before would be available and he would love to have us back. It turned out that the only change was that the trailer that was next door was gone. Lloyd found out the tenant was some kind of a traveling thug for the Ku Klux Klan. I had only met him once, but I was easily able to believe it. We were happy that we would now be alone on the farm with all its amenities.

Lloyd was among the very best kind of people. He kept his hunting dogs, his daughter's horse and about fifty pigs on the property. It was only rarely he would call to say that he or the fellow who cared for the pigs couldn't show up and asked me to wash down the pen and put feed into the troughs. It was not a big job and I was happy to help. The rent for this five-room house was $85 a month, and that was cheap even in those days. He also was always asking me to ride his daughter's horse, which needed to be exercised, and to take his dogs hunting. So, with extra benefits like these, who would complain about a little hog swilling? Not me, that's for sure.

It was rewarding to be able to work with the newbies coming through the squadron for "In Type" training before they went into harm's way in Viet Nam. Some were transitioning from fixed wing, but the majority of them were fresh out of the training command. There were a growing number of us who had walked the walk over there and were able to show them the skills and tactics that worked and how to avoid doing the things that would get them killed. When we had been in training at VMO-1, it had not been the quality of the instructors that left us not fully prepared but that they had not been in the real situation in Viet Nam, at least not during the stage of the war that was being fought then, to know what did and didn't work. However, the most important lesson we taught was always to be learning for yourself and always, always to stay ahead of both the bird and the situation that was going on around you.

Life was pretty easy now that I was one of the old salts and a captain instead of a newbie second lieutenant who didn't know his ass from his elbow. Combat-experienced UH-1E pilots were still fairly scarce at that point so we were kept pretty busy. VMO-1 had plenty of birds, and there were no budget restrictions on spending money for maintenance, ammunition or fuel.

Part of the syllabus for the trainees was *Cross Country Visual Navigation*. This was a license to ride. Anytime I wanted to go somewhere to see friends or family or to just get away, all I needed to do was find a Stud that wanted flight time and required a check-off on cross country hops. This was as hard as finding a kid that wanted to go get ice cream. With this kind of freedom I was off—here, there, and everywhere.

Many civilian fields and some military fields at that time had little or no experience with helicopters, especially helicopters with skids that didn't come rolling onto their runway and then taxi as directed just like fixed wing. UH-1Es air taxied. Air taxiing could, of course, be called flying very near the ground because that's what it was. This allowed me to get away with asking for and getting cleared to do stuff that had never been done at those fields before. For example, a call to the tower to request a landing at the flag pole often caused a long pause followed by a hesitant sounding, "You're cleared."

Flying home to Connecticut the shortest route when leaving from Quantico, where I would refuel, direct to Bradley Field in Hartford took us almost over Kennedy Airport on Long Island. There was no way I could ever get clearance through this very busy area. My solution, therefore, was to get down on the beach, call the tower when there was a break on the radio, and "report" that I was flying under their approach path at 50 feet over the beach. I got a "Roger" once and no answer the other times I used this technique. It worked and nobody was ever in any danger since the planes were still hundreds of feet above me.

I always had a curiosity about Benson Gyrocopters so I set up a cross country hop to the Raleigh-Durham airport, where their plant was located within the airport complex. Their advertisements showed a helicopter landing pad right at the plant, and it looked perfect. The Stud did his planning and off we went the next day to go gyrocopter shopping. When we arrived, I took the controls and called the tower for clearance to land on the Benson helo pad. There was a very long pause and then a tentative response that we were cleared. I then asked for directions, which caused an even longer pause. Finally they came back to tell me that they were just over the tree line, due west of the tower. I headed in that direction and soon saw an old corrugated steel hangar in an opening in the trees, and, sure enough, there was the pad. It was pretty obvious that this pad was primarily for decoration as it was one tight spot. Not too tight for a salty Viet Nam vet, however. As I started to let down from my hover over the tree tops, the workers from the factory who had come out to see what was going on looked like an anthill that had just been kicked. They were running around like crazy to slide the hangar doors shut before my rotor blast rearranged the factory's interior layout. We were one big hit and, yes, the first helicopter to land on their pad. We got the full tour of the plant and a detailed inspection of a gyrocopter. I would describe it as a lawn chair with a motor and propeller attached to a pipe with a free-wheeling rotor on top of it. When I got an offer to fly it, I had to quickly explain that I would love to but I had to get home. In reality I wouldn't have risked my life in anything as flimsy as that. We said our good-byes, they closed their doors, and I called the tower for clearance to take off from the Benson pad. Another long pause and I heard "You're cleared. Please report when you are clear of the airport." They were a small regional airport at that time so traffic was not an issue, but I am sure they were glad to have this stranger gone.

One more cross country story I can't resist. We were on our way to see a friend in Alabama and planned to refuel in Fort Benning on the Georgia-Alabama line. We were VFR (Visual Flight rules) but the weather kept getting worse with the ceiling coming down and the visibility shrinking. One of the privileges of a Naval Aviator qualified in helicopters was to operate under a flight rule called "Special VFR" (Special Visual Flight Rules). Special VFR was 300 foot ceiling and one mile visibility. Notice in the note below that the qualified pilot can make the determination himself.

Sec. 91.157—Special VFR weather minimums The determination of visibility by a pilot in accordance with paragraph (c)(2) of this section is not an official weather report or an official ground visibility report.

The worsening weather soon had us in Special VHR conditions and then soon below that. There was no alternative but to file an instrument flight plan to proceed IFR (Instrument Flight Rules). To do this we needed to get organized and we weren't going to be able to do that while flying in that goop so I landed in a large farm field. We got in the back, got out the charts, made the plan, got the frequencies, and were ready. Back into the cockpit, I called Atlanta Center and filed the instrument flight plan to Benning.

We soon were cleared and launched out of the field into the goop and on the gauges. We were handed off to Benning approach and were being vectored in when we broke out into the clear at about four hundred feet. I immediately cancelled the IFR flight plan and went back to special VFR. We were over the river that divides Georgia and Alabama and runs in a big gully about 100 feet deep and curves to the north, flowing right by the end of the Benning runway—piece of cake. We were maybe three miles down the river from the runway and had slowed to about sixty knots. Oops, there was a bridge with its top out of sight in the clouds. I climbed up, temporarily IFR, cleared the bridge and let back down into the clear. As I rounded the river bend, I called the tower for landing and they responded "We do not have you in sight." I answered, "You will in just a moment when we are at the west end of your runway." I paused and then said, "Do you have us now? We are over your runway and taxiing. Where do you want us to set down?" Another one of those long pauses until they finally gave us directions to the base operations office. "Am I cleared direct?" I asked. "Yes," they responded. Off I went over the grass, landed, shut down, and went to operations to order fuel. By now a damn fool Major had shown up, and I knew this was going to turn into some kind of big deal. After the "Who the hell are you?" and "How the hell did you get here ya-da, ya-da, ya-da?" we got the fuel and a ride to the BOQ (Bachelor Officers Quarters), after he finally learned what Special VFR was. We had a nice dinner and drinks at the club and met some nice people that night.

In the morning the weather was well below VFR minimums but well within Special VFR. I told the duty clerk I was on my way and thank-you when he said "You can't go," and phoned the Major. I will not go over all the details except how pissed off the Major was when he finally found out that a Naval Aviator has the authority to sign his own flight plan when not at a Naval Air facility.

We went on our way for a great time with my friend and his family.

Caribbean Vacation

Marine Corps Style

M y wife and I had been planning a trip home for the Christmas holidays. I had been back from Viet Nam about five months. Beverly was pregnant and we were looking forward to this holiday with our families. It was about nine o'clock at night a few days before my wife and I were to leave for Connecticut when the phone rang. It was the executive officer of the squadron saying, "Your Christmas leave has been canceled, and you will be leaving the day after tomorrow in a detachment of six H-34s and two UH-1E slicks for the Caribbean aboard the *LPH Guam*. We do not know how long this cruise will last; it could be a month or six months. I know this is very short notice and your wife and family won't be happy, but all the H-46s have been grounded worldwide due to the numbers that have been lost to mid-flight break ups. The H-46 squadron that was all set to leave has to stand down. Make your arrangements at home tonight and be in the ready room at 0700 in the morning for the briefing. Sorry about this." "Yes, sir", was all I could say as I hung up. You can imagine what happened next and that from there on it was a mad scramble to get everything ready and loaded in just two days so we could meet the boat off the coast as they steamed by on their way south. Tony Pecoraro was the pilot of the other UH-1E, but I do not remember who the crew chiefs were. One of the H-34 drivers was my long time friend Johnny Longdin. This was just another one of our many adventures together over the past four to five years.

Once we got aboard the boat we quickly realized that there was nothing that was going to change this so we may as well go with the flow. That left us a week or so with absolutely nothing to do until it was time to off-load on Vieques, a small island between Puerto Rico and St. Thomas. There was a very small Marine facility there called Camp Butler, which would be our home for the duration. We settled into our staterooms, which weren't bad living, especially as we were only a small group of pilots compared to what would normally be in this space. The H-34 drivers, and their co-pilots, of course, had gotten the same call we had gotten two days before, so their attitude was no different than ours. This made for a pretty salty group of pilots, the majority of whom were short timers counting the days before they got to go back to civilian life. For now we had fine food in the ward room, movies in the ready room, and no rank making noises between us and the leader of the H-34 group, who was also our commanding officer. This was just fine with Tony and me.

A word about the drivers of H-34s, or Dogs, as they were referred to, is called for here, since they are a breed in and of themselves. I and the rest of the Marine helicopter drivers of my vintage had time flying the H-34 in the training command so I can speak with authority when I say that this was not an easy bird to fly. It required a lot of skill and constant attention, but when flown by a skilled pilot it was a thing to behold. It would lift and

209

lift and lift, sneak in and out of match box sized LZs, and bring you and your passengers home, even when it was full of holes. You would therefore be correct to assume that the pilots on this cruise were all well seasoned and highly skilled and also had the attitude to go with it. Putting Tony and me together with these six Dog drivers and their co-pilots into a place like this cruise may not have been the best command decision ever made. No one had to doubt even one iota about the job getting done, and done well, but who was going to keep this salt-laden bunch in any semblance of proper military decorum? Nobody on this cruise, I can assure you of that.

All the pilots did come to the same realization at about five o'clock the first evening aboard. We had all forgotten about no drinking aboard ship! This caused a morale collapse and a lot of bitching and complaining in the wardroom that night. There was little that could be done so we all settled down into goof-off mode. Sometime the next day at a briefing in the ready room we learned that the ship was going to stop at Gitmo (Guantanamo Bay). This was long before it became a terrorist detention camp with all the associated stories. It is on the eastern tip of Cuba, where the guards from both sides would growl at each other across the fence that divided it from the rest of Cuba. But it was perfectly safe, even to the point that some of the Navy personnel stationed there had their families living on base with them. There were only two questions from the peanut gallery about the announcement. Will we be able to go ashore? Is there a bar? The answers were yes and yes, which brought a resounding happy shout. Maybe the recently, temporarily promoted Commodore who was in charge of the cruise was our kind of guy. He had probably heard how low the pilots' morale had become when they were forced to stop drinking and had immediately diverted us to the nearest bar. Whatever the reason, it was a very effective morale booster.

It was early in the afternoon when we arrived, and the obliging swabbies got the anchor down. All the pilots had already formed a line to disembark and were encouraging the crew to hurry with getting the gangplank down and the launches into the water. After all, we were very thirsty.

The Officers Club was very nice, with beautiful views of the Caribbean Sea, a wonderful atmosphere for a group of very salty Marine helicopter pilots in which to recover from their forced period of sobriety of almost two days by then. It didn't take very long before we realized that this club might be not be fully aware of what constituted normal behavior in clubs that are usually patronized by clientele such as ourselves. It was less than a couple of hours before we were invited to utilize the seating area outside on the patio. That allowed their other patrons, mostly dressed in white uniforms, to have intellectual conversations among themselves. That was fine with us, and the party didn't even slow down. The only thing we had to go inside for now was to use the head and to get more to drink.

It was getting on towards eight o'clock and we were all now very hungry. When someone went into the club to ask about being fed they learned that only the dining room was serving that night and the working uniforms we were wearing were not acceptable dress. One of our group approached the Commodore, who was sitting at the bar, assuming that, since he had arranged to get us to a bar so efficiently, he could get us fed as well. The only problem here was that another member of our group, who for some mysterious reason was not using all his brain cells, decided it would be great fun to get onto his hands and knees, sneak up behind the Commodore and jerk the barstool out from under him. Well, not only was this not a good idea in the first place, it resulted in the Commodore falling smack on his ass on the floor. Not only did everyone in the club think we should leave immediately, we, for the first time, were in full agreement and were already beating feet for the door except, I learned very much later, for two members who decided they did not want to leave without providing some assistance to the obliging club staff, so they helped prepare the pool area for a hurricane by throwing all the patio furniture into the pool before they arrived at the front door ready for departure.

As the group of us was waiting by the door to leave, a young Ensign dressed in whites and his wife, looking very fine indeed, came into the club. Our group pretty much came to attention, not in respect for the Ensign, of course, but for the very nice piece of gear attached to his arm. He immediately was able to ascertain that we were an alien group from another planet even though we wore the insignia denoting our status as officers and gentlemen. In his young and inexperienced mind he felt it was his responsibility to correct what he judged to be a deviation from conduct becoming an officer and a gentleman. This was a bad decision on his part, to say nothing about his timing.

One of our group members had the nickname Billy Goat. His name was derived from a dubious habit that exhibited itself when his brain cells were malfunctioning and he felt that someone had insulted him. This was fast becoming one of those times, so, with the young Ensign attempting to appear wise and authoritative in front of his wife, Billy Goat began his routine. He slowly and deliberately brought his drink to his mouth and took a big bite out of the glass. Yes, I said the glass. Uh, oh, we realized soon that this situation was going way, way out of control. The Ensign was stunned into a state of awe that left him frozen and speechless. By this time the rest of us were out the door but not too far away to miss this next bit in the drama. Billy Goat slowly positioned himself front and center on the hapless Ensign and took another bite out of his glass. He then raised his head and began to spit what was now a mouthful of blood and glass from the top of the Ensign's head to all the way down his white uniform. He then turned to the wife and said "Good evening and my compliments to you, madam." and joined us outside, where we were all in full retreat.

With some gentle guidance by the less than completely whacked out revelers in the group, we got back to the launch landing area after we determined there was no place to find a meal anywhere on the base. We boarded the launch and, as we approached the gangplank, which was rigged over the side of the ship and lit up like a Christmas tree, we could see hundreds of sharks. We all hung onto the rails like our life depended on it and hoped we were not going to be asked to walk the plank as punishment for our lack of decorum during the evening. I am sure somebody heard something from somebody the next day when the ship got back underway, but I didn't. No harm, no foul. I wonder how long the wife stayed with her Ensign after she had seen what real officers are made of. If she was smart, she is still married to him.

In a couple of days we arrived in the vicinity of Vieques and began our off-load. I am not sure why, but for some reason the Navy seemed to be even happier than we were that we were no longer going to be aboard. I wonder why that could have been. I launched with all of the crew's personal gear loaded and we headed for the strip at Camp Butler. I do not remember there being a tower controlling landings, but I sure do remember the cows that were all over the camp, including the runway. We had to hover around and herd them out of the way so we could land. It turns out that when the Marine Corps negotiated the deal for this land, the seller kept the rights to graze cattle.

After we had landed and shut down, we were directed to a Quonset hut up the hill that was to be the officers' living quarters. We weren't very impressed with what we saw, and that opinion went even further south when we actually had to chase a cow out of the building, where it was resting in the shade. The hut was divided into two sections with a head and shower in the middle. The fourteen of us moved into one half with a rack for each of us set on the concrete floor. We slid our footlockers under the racks and we were all moved into our new home.

While we are here at the hut I will relate two quick stories. The first is about "Back-ah-rude-ah". A group of four guys chartered a boat to go fishing one day. They spent the day getting sunburned and, of course, since this was not a US naval vessel and drinking was condoned, getting inebriated as well. They actually managed to catch one fish, a barracuda they affectionately named "Back-ah-rude-ah." If you are not aware, barracudas are smelly, slimy fish with a set of teeth right out of a horror movie. They are not good eating so the boat crew was going to throw it back. No way, was the unanimous vote of these salty warriors. They knew a trophy fish when they saw one and were surely going to bring it home to prove what great sportsmen they were. As you probably have already guessed, when they showed up at the hut with the smelly thing, they were not well received. In fact, they were told to get that thing out of there ASAP. Then a dose of reality struck them. What the hell are we going to do with this thing? That was not a problem for us non-fishermen so we left to eat, drink and be merry as best we could. Happy hour had arrived.

That evening we came back to the hut to get cleaned up and go to bed. I had finished and was in bed when a loud and angry yell filled the space. One of our group, the one who had been complaining the most to the fishermen earlier in the evening, found that someone had put "Back-ah-rude-ah" into his bed with a hat and a cigar clamped tightly in its teeth. There were only four people in the hut who thought this was funny and therefore immediately identified themselves as the culprits. I do not know its final resting place but it was not in the unhappy camper's bed. His crankiness over this incident carried over, however, and any activity that came close to disturbing his peaceful rest was quickly clipped in the bud.

It wasn't more than a couple of days later that we had some visitors who did not understand how important it was to listen to any suggestions made by our cranky hut mate concerning his peaceful repose. We had been flying in support of a landing exercise during the day. One of the few days we had any real work to do. Since the grunts were ashore, the officers were assigned to the other end of our hut. They were delighted to be able to take a long shower and get cleaned up after doing all that stuff grunts do to get so tired and dirty. Although non-aviation Marine officers do not even begin to approach our near professional status as drinkers, our new hut mates were fair to middling amateurs in the game. They, of course, had been unable to practice lately as they had been stuck aboard the *Guam*, where teetotaling is the rule.

They were in full swing at the other end of the hut getting soused and making a lot of noise and raising hell. Even a cranky Marine would allow some latitude for this type of activity, but after a couple of hours, and it was approaching eleven, the crankiness level was beginning to overflow in the recipient of "Back-ah-rude-ah." In fact the rest of us were also thinking that it was time for the party to end but were happy to let him take care of it. He wandered on down to the other end in his skivvies and quietly told them he thought it was time for them to go to bed. They seemed receptive and said they would be done soon. And there was some reduction in the volume and General uproar. But it slowly picked back up again and after about twenty minutes our man yelled at them in no uncertain terms to shut up, and shut up now. This caused an unpleasant response from them about a recommendation to put one body part into another. All of us others, who were lying there waiting to go to sleep, realized they had crossed the line.

The next noise we heard was a footlocker being dragged out from under a bunk. Then there was some rustling around as someone was looking for something in its depths. Next was the unmistakable sound of a magazine being loaded into a 45 and the action being pulled back and a round being chambered. Uh, oh; they've done it now. I managed to squeeze myself down into the bunk and was holding my breath. He didn't give a warning, just shot a round right down the length of the hut. In the ensuing silence, while all ears were ringing, he calmly said, "I asked you nice, and then I asked again. Now you have been told. I assume you have no questions." There was not a single peep. After a minute I heard the magazine come out of the weapon, the chamber unloaded, and then the footlocker being slid back under the bunk. I slept soundly the rest of the night.

The daily routine was pretty slow. There was not much call for us unless the ground troops were going to be doing a practice assault. We had some VIP hops and some bring this here or that there requests, but in General we would have rather been flying more. Soon after we had gotten settled in, a liberty schedule was established. This could not have worked out better for Tony and me. Each day at 4:00 PM one UH-1E was to take six passengers on liberty. They were to return on or before 8:00 AM the next morning. You would think that a schedule like this must have been set up by Tony and me, but we just fell into it. What a deal this was. I don't remember how the schedule was worked out for the H-34 pilots, co-pilots and the enlisted men, but for Tony and me it meant we were on liberty every other night. My only preparation was to put my flight suit on over my civilian clothes and grab my toilet kit, and I was good to go. We got to choose whether we were going to San Juan, St. Thomas or St. Croix. The furthest away was San Juan at about sixty miles, with St. Thomas just twenty miles away. I went to St. Croix once, but there was not much there so never went back. San Juan offered free lodging at the Coast Guard station, which was nice, but when it came to a good party, St. Thomas was hard to beat. San Juan did offer enjoyable evenings but there was only limited opportunity for grab ass activities and none of the great opportunities we were handed by a few of our more adventurous enlisted men when they were in St. Thomas.

On the San Juan runs I liked to fly along the beach. There were only two or three hotels there then. I would round Moro Castle into the harbor and land at the Coast Guard station, which was, at that time, located on the southeast end where the commercial docks are now. This whole approach left me below the bluffs of the Castle so when I called for landing they still couldn't see me. The first couple of times they would come back with a "we do not have you in sight" type response. So, as I came around the corner at ninety knots in about a 60° bank, I would call again asking if they had me now rounding Moro Castle. "We have you and you are cleared to land," they responded. After they had gotten the idea, I got cleared before I began the turn even though they couldn't see me. This was a pretty limited amount of fun for that thirty to forty minute trip so I came up with a little added attraction for my passengers on a couple of the runs. When I got to one of the high rise hotels, I came into a hover and would go up and down and side to side to see what we could get to come out onto the balconies. We were one of the better tourist attractions for the day so we usually got a fair sized crowd in attendance. As you can imagine, the passengers thought this was an excellent addition to the normally boring ride. They would also be vigorously pulling up their shirts in the universal sign for "Show me your tits" whenever a woman came out. In the late sixties we got a fair number of takers, which caused much hooting and hollering from all on board and seemed to help set the tone for the evening's debauchery.

We learned one other neat and money-saving tourist tip about San Juan. The cruise liners docked in the harbor under Moro Castle were always delighted to oblige servicemen and allowed us to come aboard and go to the crew lounge and get drinks for a ridiculously low price. This allowed us to nurse that expensive nightclub beer while in the tourist traps.

The most interesting times in St. Thomas were not those sitting in the Palm Passage sipping banana daiquiris. But I must tell you that I had never had one of these before and do believe it is the absolute nicest way to get alcohol past your lips and into your waiting brain cells. Just the thought of that setting and the taste of those drinks bring me joy and happiness. Johnny Longdin and I whiled

219

away a number of tropical evenings in this fine pastime. It was the makings for this delightful concoction that constituted a Major portion of my smuggled cargo, which I will tell you about later.

One morning Johnny and I showed up at the airport ready to go home and noticed right away that there was tension and concern among the liberty party waiting to fly back with us. "What's up, guys?" I asked. "Pfc. Schmuckatello (my name for any Marine displaying behavior based on stupidity) has not shown up and nobody has seen him," was the answer. "Okay. I'll preflight and get the bird started, and maybe he will show," I said, as I got my fight suit and helmet out of the cockpit. I was ready. We waited an extra five minutes. No Schmuckatello, so I called for takeoff and we left for Vieques.

When I got the yellow sheet finished, Johnny and I went to the section to let them know we had left a man on St. Thomas. It was not news to them because they had gotten a call very late the night before from the police in St. Thomas informing them that they had arrested one Pfc. Schmuckatello for assault and battery and were holding him in their jail awaiting a hearing before the judge. Johnny and I were immediately appointed as the task force legal officers and given our first assignment. Go back to St. Thomas, find out what the hell is going on, and get it straightened out. We got showered and into our uniforms. I pulled my flight suit on and off we went.

We got a taxi to the police station, which was up on the hill overlooking the harbor. In the complex with the police were the court, the prosecutor's office and the jail. Of course neither of us had any idea of what we were supposed to do or how any of this process worked. But we quickly learned that everyone we met was great and showed us what to do, step by step.

First the detective and the arresting officers told us what the story was. You won't believe it at first, and neither did we, but it was so off the wall nobody could have made it up. Our boy Schmuckatello had made a financial arrangement with a visiting tourist from New York City. The deal being that the tourist would pay Schmuckatello the grand sum of fifty dollars for performing a very intimate act that would require him to appear to be praying while doing it. Got your attention yet? The police sure had ours. When the service was completed to the satisfaction of the tourist, he began to make payment by writing a check. We now knew Schmuckatello was very dumb, as well as leaning to a set of preferences that in that day and age were absolutely, positively unacceptable. But he was not so dumb as to think a check was going to be proper payment, and he demanded cash. The disagreement got heated very quickly so Schmuckatello made a brilliant decision and hit his customer in the head with a stool, which caused significant injury and copious quantities of blood. The tourist and some of his friends called the police, who quickly arrived, assessed the situation, and arrested Schmuckatello.

Well, well, well! The police told us our next step was to meet with the prosecutor. However, he was at a meeting and wouldn't be available for an hour, so they asked if we would like to talk with the prisoner, which, of course, we did. We were led into the jail, which was built in the Fifteenth or Sixteenth Century. It had stone floors, walls and ceilings that were dripping with moisture, rusted wrought iron bars, and malodorous smells that were incredible. You could feel the ghosts of pirates rattling their bones in the place. The police were merciful enough to have locked our Marine up in a cell by himself with a bucket to pee in and some water. He was one sad sack, a scared and contrite Marine. He knew he was in deep trouble; he just didn't know how deep it was. You can bet we didn't give him any slack. We had no idea what was going to happen to him, and chances were he would be there in jail long after we had left for home. This was no minor scrape like a bar fight that would blow over in the light of day.

Johnny and I were realizing this was serious stuff, and we needed to be minding our Ps and Qs. The prosecutor was another great guy and explained the potential punishment if convicted. He also let us know that the tourist, on the advice of his friends, had left the island early that morning for New York, and they thought he would not be returning of his own accord. With these facts on the table he confided to us that they were not very excited about moving forward with the case. He asked if we felt the Marine Corps would be able to deal with disciplining Schmuckatello. We assured him that was something he could count on. He asked if we would like to go to lunch with him since his staff would have to do some paperwork for us to take to the judge to finish this up. We learned a lot about the comings and goings of St. Thomas during lunch. Things the average tourists don't find out about.

After lunch the three of us met with the judge in his office. He got the short version of the story, agreed with the recommendation, and called the police to bring Schmuckatello to his office. The judge asked a few questions of Johnny and me about Viet Nam while we waited. When Schmuckatello arrived, the judge read him the riot act and told him he was very lucky he wasn't going to be spending time in jail and that these two fine officers had assured him the Marine Corps would deal with him appropriately.

We left with Schmuckatello in tow, flew back to Vieques and deposited him with Admin. I have no idea what happened to him. He was gone from our group, and probably the rest of his enlistment was very short. We did have a good story at happy hour, however.

It was less than a week later that Johnny and I got a message to report to Admin. He and I had not been on liberty that night so we were not aware that three of the liberty party had not returned that morning from St. Thomas. Calls determined that, sure enough, they were in jail, too. We were now the only two experienced and well-qualified legal officers in the group, so there was no question of whom to call. The dynamic duo was back in action.

Our arrival back at the police station was like seeing old friends again. We followed the same routine, getting the story from the detective and arresting officer. It seems that at about ten o'clock the night before these inebriated three had decided they needed to take a tour of the island. To accomplish this they looked for available transportation and quickly discovered a Volkswagen parked at the curb just outside the bar they had just left on one of the streets that went up to the top of the island. Possessing mechanical skills, they thought that it would be easy to hot wire and that they could then coast down the hill and pop the clutch to get it started.

The plan was quickly put into effect; the wiring modification was made, and all three hopped in and started to coast down the hill. They got about five feet and the VW jumped the curb and was heading further off the road. The passenger-types immediately started providing advice on how to steer a car in a straight line. There was just one problem they were not prepared to deal with—the locked steering column. This obstacle forced a rapid change in plan. They decided to push the car back to its original spot so nobody would know anything had happened. Just at that point the police showed up. "What's going on here, fellows?", they asked. With a little hemming and hawing and shuffling of feet, the "quicker and more brilliant" of the trio explained, "This car was rolling down the hill and we were able to get it stopped." The hardest part of this whole story to believe is that the police didn't die from laughing. Well, it got a little harder to explain when the hot wire was discovered and when the issue of the wheels being locked in a turning position made it plain that the car couldn't have rolled very far because of the way the wheels were aimed. So off to jail they went. Johnny and I were greatly relieved that this was a grab ass case compared to our initial experience.

Next stop the prosecutor's office. He told us he hoped we could help him out with this case so he could make it disappear. We, of course, were delighted to oblige. He told us that the owner of the VW was the fellow who owned the bar where our boys had been drinking. He gave us his name and directions and said he usually got in about noon. We walked up to the bar and asked for him. He wasn't in yet so we, of course, had to have a beer while we waited. It wasn't long before he showed up, walked over, said *Semper Fi*, and asked what he could do for us. Things were looking up, way up. We quickly became confident that we could work this out, Marine to Marine. When he heard the story the three of them had told, we all got to laughing our asses off at how stupid these clowns were. Bottom line: since there was no damage to the car, he dropped the complaint and even paid for our beers and lunch. We assured him that they would get Captain's Mast (non-judicial punishment). He called the prosecutor to tell him this and we went back to get our wayward Marines.

They were very glad to see us standing outside their dank cell. We told them to shut their mouths and only say thank you to everybody we saw on our way out of there.

When we had all gotten aboard and taken off, it seemed as if there was still some misguided hope in this group that they were going to wiggle out of this entirely. Their designated mouth-piece started to explain about the runaway car and how this was all a big mistake. He got about fifteen seconds into it, and I told him he was damn lucky we had gotten them out of this jam and, if he continued insulting my intelligence by saying anything other than thank you for getting us out of this mess and apologizing for their stupidity, I would see that their punishment would increase dramatically. I watched as the other two nodded vigorously to indicate that their buddy should shut up. I then heard thank you and I'm sorry three times and not another word after that. We needed these guys, who were crew chiefs, to help work our mission. They had to suffer their punishment and also be the butt of many jokes from all their friends and, of course, no more liberty. The legal department of Boden & Longdin had done a great job again.

It had been explained to each of us, not long after we had arrived on Vieques, that each man could bring home two bottles of liquor, which was the duty free limit at that time. To keep this under control the CO had a conex box (shipping container) designated for us to keep our liquor in. It would be cleared through customs all at one time, and we could pick up our two bottles the day after we arrived back home.

Two bottles—you have got to be kidding me. With the fantastic prices in St. Thomas and it being the only source I knew for banana liqueur, a required ingredient for our favorite Banana Daiquiris, I needed a better plan. There was one other challenge that had reared its ugly head concerning the payment of duty. When my wife and I were married, we only received one place setting of the china service all brides so carefully agonized over during their wedding planning. Someone, a woman I am sure, had blabbed to my wife the information that you could buy china at great discounts in St. Thomas. To that end she sent me all the specifications and her burning desire to own twelve complete place settings as well as a long list of accessory pieces. You can imagine that this brought joy to my heart, I being so enamored of the idea of possessing a completed set of fine china. But, if this is what she wanted, so be it.

This was going to need an accomplice or two. The crew chief and Johnny were on board as soon as I explained what we had to do, since they, too, could have the benefit of a sufficient supply of fine liquor at bargain prices for themselves. I probably did not mention the detail about the china to the abetting parties at this point. The first step was to buy the booze and the china, which, to my dismay, I found was available for purchase, and get it to Vieques. The second thing we needed to do was to make up a fake mission for the legal team. This was easy. We just told the CO that on our last liberty run to St. Thomas the judge and district attorney had contacted us and wanted to meet us in their office just prior to our leaving the area. They wanted to make sure there were no more issues that needed to be resolved. So on the day before we were to on-load back aboard the *Guam* for our return to MCAS New River, on a regular liberty run we purchased the goods, including the china, had it all repacked into plain boxes, and had them store it ready to be delivered to the airport on the afternoon of our "appointment with the judge and the district attorney."

The plan to go back aboard the *Guam* required that all of the unit's gear be brought and stacked next to the runway so everything could be loaded on the H-34s or carried as sling loads the next morning. All the crews' and pilots' personal gear was to be stored aboard their own birds and remain on board until the first landing in MCAS New River to avoid loss, a plan that fit in nicely with ours. A couple of days before we were to leave, we three conspirators dutifully took our two bottles of booze with the proper labels to the conex box to be stored with everyone else's. We didn't want anybody to think we were foolish enough to not take advantage of this bargain. They might have thought there was something wrong with us or, even worse, smelled a rat.

The final day arrived and everyone was excited about going home. The three of us packed our personal gear on board my bird prior to leaving for our "meeting" and headed for St. Thomas. We had a nice leisurely lunch, and then went to collect our goods and ride with them to the airport. We got the truck cleared onto the parking apron and loaded the bird. We were able to get everything neatly tucked here and there and then neatly arranged our personal gear so everything looked like it belonged there.

We took off for Vieques and landed at the far end of the line of birds that were all set and ready for the next morning. We all had a great going-away party and went to bed early. They wanted the two UH-1Es to come aboard first so they could get us down the elevator and stored in the back of the hangar deck. That way they would be out of the way during all the flights the H-34s would be making to bring on the tons and tons of gear and personnel, again fitting our plans perfectly. The H-34s had most of the work when it came to hauling gear, which was what they did best.

The plan was to leave everything in our birds, which would then be all ready to go ashore in New River. So by mid-morning our two birds were snug as a bug and well out of anyone's prying eyes and the crew chief would be the only one to have any reason to check on his bird. As you will see, the weather pretty much kept everybody off the hangar deck on the way home, anyway. Even as the on-load was under way, the *Guam* started the run for home and we got set to goof off for a few days.

The next morning we started to get roughed up, and that round-bottomed bathtub called a ship could roll like a hammock. By the end of the day we were taking green water over the bow of that 600 foot LPH, whose flight deck was about fifty feet high. This was rough water in anybody's book and we had to slow down, thus adding time to the trip. There were seasick people everywhere you looked. The wardroom was nearly empty and they had to wet the tablecloths to keep everything from sliding off onto the deck. For a few of us old salts it meant we had the run of the ship and nobody to bother us.

There was one activity for which I had to limit myself to about one hour at a time before I had to head for my bunk and lie down. That was watching a movie. It was not that the ready room, where the movies were shown, was just under the flight deck and high on the rolling arc; it was the movie screen that got to me. It was a pull-down type attached to the overhead, facing athwartship. This meant that the screen hung vertically like a pendulum while the ship rolled under it. The projector was, of course, attached to the ship, so the result was that the picture on the screen got larger and then smaller with each roll. Think about it; it was tough to even get through an hour.

After two to three days the ship finally got us to more reasonable weather and calmer seas as we approached the North Carolina coast. They got all the birds on deck with the initial loads that would be taken ashore. Again, getting the UH-1Es off first was the plan. I had to ask Tony to be sure to take a little tour around the New River area before he went back into land. I suggested he might want to fly over his house and say hello to his wife; just don't ask why. Stall for about fifteen minutes and we can join up a couple of miles south of the runway and go in together. I could tell this was going to cost us a couple of bottles in the end, but he didn't need to know anything more at this point.

As we neared New River, the winter weather in North Carolina made us quickly realize that things were not bad in the sunny Virgin Islands and what we at first had thought was going to be a grind, had turned out to be a hell of a lot of fun. We were now almost back to being short timers and counting the days until we could get out.

I launched from the *Guam* for what I hoped would be the last time and headed south of MCAS New River and directly to the farm where I lived to the west of the base and off the end of a dirt road. Part of the farm consisted of a large field surrounded by woodland. No one was going to see anything or find our contraband before I could get home and secure it. It took just a moment or two for the crew chief to get the boxes unloaded, and we were off to meet Tony, land, and go through Customs, which would be there to meet us.

I was home again after a couple of months with a happy wife, cheap booze, and more good stories to laugh about while we drank it.

USS Guam LPH9

Cow Evicted From Our Barracks

Tony Pecoraro

More information and photos at
www.klondikeplayboy.com

Mustering Out

The last day finally arrived. July 1, 1968. Just over five years of active duty. Two years longer than I had originally signed up for, but a better deal I could not have made. The recruiter back in Middletown was right. The Marine Corps does not make deals. I did what I was told and ended up way ahead of where I would have been if I had taken one of the deals that the other services had offered me. Just because I had so much fun does not mean I didn't give the Marine Corps the best that I had. And they in return gave me the best that they had. The Corps' respect for the Marine and the Marine's respect for the Corps is the reason that "Once a Marine, always a Marine" is true.

With our brand new baby son, timed to be born just before my discharge, and all our gear in the moving van, we started home to Connecticut. No more uniforms, no more inspections, and the prospect of a completely new life was unfolding before me. In the last five years I had grown from a boy to a man. I had lived with a very high level of responsibility that had had a significant impact on the lives of others and it now felt normal to me. At that point I did not realize that this chapter of my life was closing and that I would almost never again be asked or expected to achieve at the levels I had already reached by twenty-five years of age.

The new life started with no thoughts of failure or problems. I could overcome whatever came along. I was given a small test early on when, with the moving van behind us to unload the furniture, we discovered that the cellar of our new apartment was full of water. There were no cell phones or Instant Messaging in those days so I couldn't summon help to solve the problem for me. So, off we went, with the moving van in tow and its driver not sure what he was getting into, to search for a new home that we could move into, right then. Within the hour we found a brand new duplex with a "For Rent" sign in the window. It looked great as we peered through the widows and it was located near the highway to school and to work. My wife stayed there with the movers while I went to a phone booth to call the number on the sign. I got the builder, went to his house, gave him a check, got the keys and returned in less than an hour. I opened the door, the movers brought in the furniture, and we were home—another dragon slain. I will have to say that my parents thought the rent of $185 per month for the new place was too expensive, more than double what we had been paying. It was, however, the exact amount of my monthly GI Bill payment for school tuition.

I worked between thirty and forty hours a week while I finished three years of college in two years. The University of New Haven allowed veterans to register for classes before other students, one of the main reasons I chose them. This meant I was able to either have all my classes in three mornings a week or all day long for two days a week. I carried eighteen credit hours except for one semester when I took twenty one hours. I also took classes in the summer. I graduated magna cum laude in

June 1970. There was surely a big difference in the way I attacked my education after I had gotten "straightened out" than before.

During the last semester of school, I started to build our house. As soon as I graduated I was able to work on the house every night after work. We moved into it by the end of that summer. It was then I began to settle into the rest of my life. A new pace that was more "normal" and slower but was, unnoticed, also drawing me further and further from the edge. Jobs, school board, civic duties, another child, a move to Florida, a divorce, a second marriage, and then one day I got my Medicare card in the mail. I couldn't believe it. How the hell did this happen? It had been forty years since I had lived the incredible experiences of Viet Nam. The forty years had been good to me. I had had fun, prospered, reared fine children, and made great friends, but this life had been lived very far from the edge, the edge of life that had been so near, so fulfilling and so meaningful during the years in the Marine Corps. The years when the vitality and the impact I made were so real you could taste it and feel it.

There were others who had shared this life on the edge with me, but I had lost almost all contact with them. My friends and comrades from the Marine Corps and I had all gone our separate ways. It was many, many years since I had given almost any thought at all to the days that were now so long ago. The absence of recalling and telling the stories made them fade. When I did think about them, I began to doubt my memory. Maybe it wasn't really like that; maybe time had let the memories grow to seem bigger than they should be; maybe I was just kidding myself.

It wasn't until the mid-1990s that I went to a Viet Nam Marine Helicopter and Crew Association (Pop-A-Smoke) reunion and made my first reconnection. It was not very long after I first came onto the beach in Pensacola on that cold and rainy day of my first reunion that the doubt was wiped away. We looked each other in the eye, gave a little nod and a smile, and we knew it had happened, it was real, and we damn well did do it. Not only that; with the nod and the look we were giving each other permission to be proud of what we had done.

It was the pride that had been missing. The pride that allows you to own the value of what you do. Being able to be proud was slowly returning to many of us Viet Nam veterans. At the same time, the General population's attitude was also changing. Maybe it was a stupid, goddamned war, but there were a hell of lot of good men doing things for each other day in and day out. Slowly we could let our light come out from under our bushel and acknowledge a sense of pride in what we had done. People actually said, "Thank-you," and we could say, "You're welcome."

God bless all those, and especially my very dear friend John Harding, a Marine grunt whom I met many years after Viet Nam while sailing in the Bahamas, who were never able to feel the pride, whose personal demons about their Viet Nam experience were too much for them to bear, and who took their own lives as their only way to escape. God damn the war.

God damn all wars.

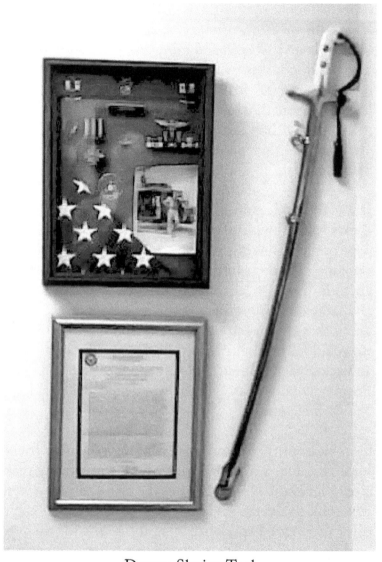

Dragon Slaying Tool

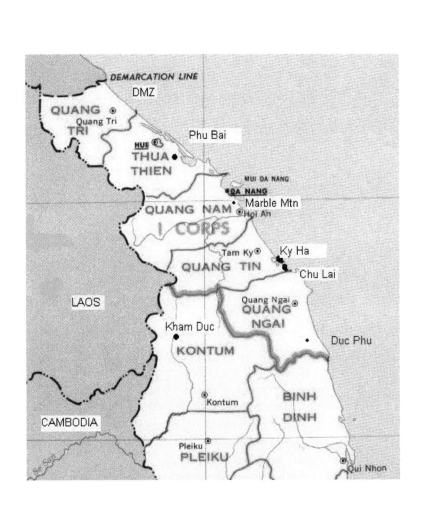

Glossary

ARVN	Army of the Republic of Viet Nam
BOQ	Bachelor Officers Quarters
Bingo	Minimum fuel needed to return to Carrier or Safe Field or base
CO	Commanding Officer
Collective	Controlled rotor blade pitch for lift
Cyclic	Controlled the rotor plane to go forward, back and sideways
DASC	Direct Air Support Center
DFC	Distinguished Flying Cross
DI	Drill Instructor
DMZ	Demilitarized Zone
FAC	Forward Air Controller
FAM-1	First Familiarization Flight
G's	Gravitational forces, negative and positive, when flying
GCA	Ground Controlled Approach
Guard Channel	Frequency monitored by aircraft to declaring emergencies
Grunts	Infantry Marines
HUEY	UH-1
I-Corp	Northern most military zone in Viet Nam (called i-Corp)
II-Corp	Next zone to the south (this and others called 2,3 Corp etc.)
IFR	Instrument Flight Rules
KIA	Killed in Action

LPH	Landing Platform Helicopter as in LPH USS Guam
LZ	Landing Zone
MACV	Military Assistance Command Viet Nam
Magneto	Aircraft piston engine ignition system
MARCAD	Marine Cadet
MCAS	Marine Corps Air Station
NAS	Naval Air Station
NAVCAD	Navy Cadet
NVA	North Vietnam Army
PMIP	Post Maintenance Check Pilot
PT	Physical Training
PTSD	Post Traumatic Stress Disorder
R&R	Rest and Recreation
ROK	Republic of Korea
Rudders	Controlled the tail rotor to counter torque and heading
SAR	Search and Rescue
Skivvies	Underwear
Slick	UH-1E without guns and rockets
SOG	Studies and Observation Group (often erroneously called Special Operations Group)
TACA	Tactical Air Coordinator Airborne
TACAN	Tactical Air Navigation
UH-1E	Utility Helicopter, model 1 version E
VC	Viet Cong
VFR	Visual Flight Rules
VMO-6	Squadron Designation V = Fixed Wing, M = Marine, O = Observation, 6 = 6th (VMO squadrons used to fly Cessna O-1Cs, the reason for the V)

WIA   Wounded in Action
Winger Number The Numerical order of Naval Aviator
                        Designation
XO   Executive Officer
Yellow Sheet   The aircraft's flight and maintenance
                        records

T-34 MENTOR
Beechcraft

Specifications

Wing span: 32 feet 10 inches
Length: 25 feet 10 inches
Height: 9 feet 7 inches
Speed: maximum: 162 knots
Ceiling: 18,600 feet
Range: maximum: 755 nautical miles
Power plant: Continental 0-470-4 engine
Crew: one instructor, one student

T-28 Trojan
North American Aviation

Specifications

Crew: Two
Length: 33 ft 0 in (10.06 m)
Wingspan: 40 ft 1 in (12.22 m)
Height: 12 ft 8 in (3.86 m)
Wing area: 268 ft² (24.9 m²)
Empty weight: 6,424 lb (2,914 kg)
Max takeoff weight: 8,500 lb (10,500 with combat stores) (3,856 kg)
Power plant: 1× Wright R-1820-86 Cyclone radial engine, 1,425 hp (1,063 kW)
Maximum speed: 343 kn (552 km/h)
Service ceiling: 39,000 ft (10,820 m)
Rate of climb: 4,000 fpm ()

Armament

2 or 6 × wing-mounted pylons capable of carrying bombs, napalm, rockets. machine gun pods containing.30 in (7.62 mm) (training),.50 in (D-model) or twin pods with.50 in (12.7 mm) and 20 mm (.79 in) cannon (Fennec)

H-13 Sioux
Bell

Specifications

Engine: Avco Lycoming VO-435 265 HP
Rotor Diameter: 37 feet, 1.5 Inches
Length: 31 feet, 7 inches
Height: 9 feet, 3 inches
Max Takeoff Weigh: 2,950 pounds
Manufacturer: Bell Helicopter
Total Built: Over 5,000
First Built: 1948
Maximum Speed: 85 m.p.h.
Range: 256 miles
Service Ceiling: 10,500 feet

H-34D Seahorse (DOG)
Sikorsky

Specifications

Crew: 2
Capacity: 16 troops or 8 stretchers
Length: 56 ft 8.5 in
Rotor diameter: 56 ft 0 in
Height: 15 ft 11 in
Disc area: 2,463 ft²
Empty weight: 7,900 lb
Max takeoff weight: 14,000 lb Power
Wright R-1820-84 radial engine, 1,525 hp
Maximum speed: 123 mph
Range: 182 mi

UH-1E Iroquois (HUEY)
Bell

Engine: Lycoming T-53-L-11D
Fuel: Grade JP-4, JP-5, or see U.S. Navy NAVAIR
01-110HCA-1 for substitute and emergency fuels.

Engine Limits:
Max. Continuous   (900 HP)   6600 (RPM)   620° C
30 Min. Operation   (1,000 HP)   6600 (RPM)   620-640°C
Maximum Allowable (1,100 HP)   6600 (RPM)   640°C

Rotor Limits:

Power Off	*Power On*
Maximum 339 RPM	Maximum 324 RPM
Minimum 295 RPM	Minimum 294 RPM
Continuous Operation	294-324 RPM

Airspeed Limits:

Never Exceed 140 knots up to and including 6600 lb G.W. Sea level to 2000 ft. Sideward and rearward flight airspeed limitation 30 knots.

Center of Gravity Range:

Most forward C.G. up to	8150 lb G.W.	Fuse Sta. 125.0
Most forward C.G. at	8,500 lb G.W.	Fuse Sta. 125.5
Most forward C.G at	9,500 lb G.W.	Fuse Sta. 126.7
Most aft C.G. up to	7,000 lb G.W.	Fuse. Sta. 138.0
Most aft C.G. at	8,500 lb G.W.	Fuse. Sta. 134.4
Most aft C.G. at	9,500 lb G.W.	Fuse Sta. 132.0
Most aft C.G. at	Empty Weight.	Range: (+125.0) to (+138.0)

Maximum Weight:	9,500 lb all conditions.
Minimum Crew:	1 (pilot) for VFR flight.
Fuel Capacity:	242 U.S. Gallons
Oil Capacity:	3.25 U.S. Gallons

For Rotor Blade rigging information refer to U.S. Navy Technical Manual NAVAIR 01

Lightning Source UK Ltd.
Milton Keynes UK
UKHW012123011219
354576UK00001B/160/P